Classic Norway

Climbs, Scrambles
and Walks in Romsdal

cordee

First edition 1970, Cicerone Press
Revised second edition 1979, Cicerone Press
Revised third edition 1998, n.o.m.a.d.s.
Revised fourth edition with new introduction, walks and other major changes, 2005

This edition published by Cordee Ltd, 3a de Montfort Street, Leicester LE1 7HD, England

Printed in Italy

ISBN 1 904207 24 3

A catalogue record for this book is available from the British Library

Editorial, design and production management by
Outcrop Publishing Services Ltd, Cumbria

The contents of this book were believed to be correct at the time of printing. Nevertheless, the author, the publishers and their agents cannot be held resposible for any errors or ommissions, or for changes in the details given in this book, or for the consequences of any reliance on the information it provides. This does not affect your statutory rights. We have made every effort to ensure the accuracy of this guide but the landscape is always changing so we welcome any feedback readers may have. Email your comments to info@cordee.co.uk.

For maps and other guides to Norway and the rest of the world visit www.cordee.co.uk

Picture Credits
Di Taylor: page 8; Øyvind Heen: pages 9, 15, 28, 29, 31, 36, 39, 46, 47, 48, 55, 64, 74, 76, 115, 126, front cover main, front flap c; Geir Kleopaker, Åndalsnes Foto: pages 13, 22, front flap a; E Birkeland a/s: page 16; Kyrre Østbø: pages 21, 50, 70, 100, 132; Iver Gjelstenli: pages 25, 42, 139, 140, back cover; Howard Collection: pages 4, 26, 57. 106, 128; Heidi-Beate Linneweh, Åndalsnes Foto: page 44; Fred Husøy: pages 58, 60, 83, front flap d; Lars Rikard Morstøl: pages 95, 130; Bjørn Magne Øverås: page 136; James Baxter: page 138; Bernd Linneweh, Åndalsnes Foto: front flap b

Classic Norway

Climbs, Scrambles and Walks in Romsdal

Tony Howard

ROMSDAL

N O R W A Y

WALKS

AND CLIMBS

IN ROMSDAL

by TONY HOWARD

Cover artwork from the 1998 edition

Contents

Foreword

Important Notes on 2005 Edition	7
Romsdal – Joe Brown	8
Romsdal – Yves Boussard	8
Author's Acknowledgements	10

Introduction

Introduction	12
Åndalsnes, The Alpine Village by the Fjord – Odd Meringdal	13
Geology, Flora and Fauna – Børre I Grønningsaeter	14
Historical (to 1970) – Arne Randers Heen	16
Historical (from 1970) – Tony Howard	18
Travel	18
Amenities and Guiding Services	20
Entertainment	20
Accommodation	21
Local Attitude	23
Weather	23
General Equipment	24
Bivouac Equipment	25
Snow and Ice	25
Rock	26
Mountain Rescue	27
Maps, Guidebooks and Mountain Info	27
Gradings and Descriptions of Routes	29

Graded List of Climbs, Walks and Scrambles

The Routes

Lake Eikesdal Ranges	36
The Isfjord Ranges	44
The Vengetind Group	48
The Romsdalshorn Group	55
The Trolltind Group	76
The Kongen Group	115
The Finnan Group	128
The Western Ranges	132
The Southern Ranges and Dovrefjell	136
Winter Ice-Climbs	139

Appendices

Some Useful Anglo-Norwegian Words	141
Index of Peaks	142
Picture Credits	144

Romsdal and Surrounding Area

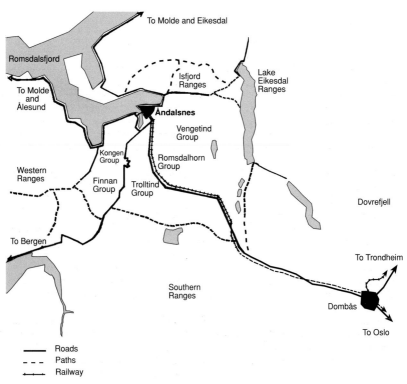

To Molde and Eikesdal

Romsdalsfjord

Isfjord Ranges

Lake Eikesdal Ranges

To Molde and Ålesund

Åndalsnes

Vengetind Group

Kongen Group

Romsdalhorn Group

Western Ranges

Finnan Group

Trolltind Group

Dovrefjell

To Bergen

To Trondheim

Southern Ranges

Dombås

To Oslo

——— Roads
- - - Paths
+-+-+ Railway

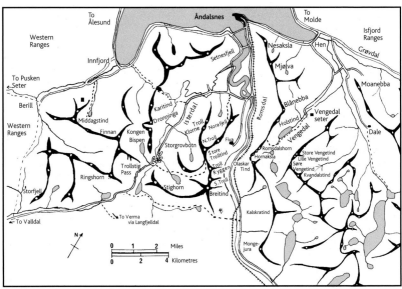

Åndalsnes

To Ålesund

To Molde

Isfjord Ranges

Western Ranges

Innfjord

Nesaksla

Hen

Grøvdal

Setnesfjell

Mjølva

To Pusken Seter

Moanebba

Berill

Karitind

Romsdal

Blånebba

Vengedal seter

Western Ranges

Middagstind

Dronninga

Isterdal

Troll

Klorne

Nora fjell

N.Troll

Holstind

Vengedal

Dale

Finnan

Kongen

Bispen

Storgrovbotn

Fiva

S.tore Trolltind

Romsdalshorn

Hornaksla

Store Vengetind

Lille Vengetind

Søre Vengetind

Olaskar Tind

Ringshorn

Trollstig Pass

Troll Ryggen

S.Troll

Kvandalstind

Storfjell

Stighorn

Breitind

To Valldal

To Verma via Langfjelldal

Kalskratind

N

0 1 2 Miles

0 2 4 Kilometres

Mongejura

Foreword

Important Notes on 2005 Edition

Ever since the second (1979) edition went out of print in the late '80s, I was regularly asked for route information on Romsdal. This resulted in the publication of the 1997 edition. When that too went out of print in 2003, I was not too concerned as by that time the Norwegians had themselves published a climbing guide to the area (*Klatring i Romsdal*, see the section headed 'Maps and Guide and info on Norway'). However, not only did the UK demand still continue but, in July 2003, whilst I was at the Romsdal Mountain Festival, numerous people pointed out that there was still a need for the 'original' guide as it not only included all the classics but was in English, making it useful to most visiting climbers. Furthermore, there are routes in it that are not in the Norwegian guide, which is more selective. It was at the Mountain Festival that the concept of 'Classic' walks and climbs in Romsdal was first mentioned, rather than simply 'Walks and Climbs' inspiring me to revise the book once more, for a fourth edition, which Cordee were kind enough to support.

This book is therefore a personal effort to provide climbers and walkers with the information needed to enjoy the original classic walks, scrambles and climbs in the mountains of Romsdal. Like its predecessor, the 1997 edition, it is mostly a straight reprint of the earlier editions, but with the 'Introductory' section updated and additional info on routes both old and new added where necessary (though I have tried to keep the 'feel' of the original 1970 edition). What are not included in this guide are the more modern climbs, for which topos will be found in the Norwegian guide, which makes an admirable companion to this guide for those seeking harder routes.

As for Romsdal itself, Åndalsnes has grown considerably, and the roads have improved. Up in the mountains, the routes remain predominantly the same as they were when we first climbed there in the 1960s, apart from less snow and the occasional rock fall (both probably due to global warming, the latter occurring most devastatingly on the Troll Wall). Grading systems have, however, changed over the years and climbing skills and equipment improved so some of the harder routes need less aid. New grades are given if an old aid or mixed route has now been done free. The section headed 'Gradings and Descriptions of Routes' should be self explanatory and should give the reader a good idea what to expect.

Romsdal's weather, as one would expect not too far from the Arctic Circle, can be variable, though the sun smiled on us most days of our last two visits to Norway. Even during the week of the July 2003 Mountain Festival, when the weather was sometimes overcast, all the popular summits were climbed and numerous walks enjoyed amongst stunning mountain and fjord scenery.

It has to be said that Norway in general and Romsdal in particular have some of the most spectacular mountains in Europe yet they are, surprisingly in this day and age, still comparatively quiet. In 1970, Odd Meringdal, then Tourist Director of Romsdal wrote 'For all the growing popularity of the area, up in the mountains it is still unusual to see other people. Perhaps, for mountaineers, we are the first and last haven in Europe for those who still seek that serenity of perfect peace and quiet which only mountains can afford'.

I am happy to say little has changed – if you want to escape the crowds, enjoy the continuous summer daylight and do some classic walks and scrambles in majestic mountain scenery, enjoy some bouldering or get some great climbs done on roadside crags, high mountains or big walls, this is the place for you!

Tony Howard, Greenfield, 2004

Romsdal
Joe Brown, Llanberis, 1970

During the past twenty years the greatest change that has taken place in the mountains isn't so much the rise in the standard of climbing, but the sheer increase in numbers of visitors to mountain areas throughout Europe. Unfortunately, this increase has been accompanied by an even more obvious increase in antisocial behaviour in the popular centres, which has understandably antagonised local residents, and the ill feeling which has been built up in several Alpine resorts will take years to live down if at all.

Fortunately, this state of affairs does not exist in Norway. Even the most popular climbing centres have few visitors. Visiting climbers quickly get to know one another and the local inhabitants, who are the most friendly and hospitable people I have ever met. It is inevitable that year by year more and more people will go to Norway in preference to the Western Alps. I hope that they will feel that the present happy relationship between climbers and residents is worth preserving at all costs, and behave accordingly.

For pure rock climbing, Norway has no equal. Many of the climbs start at two or three hundred feet above sea level and finish at a height of over five thousand feet. The descents from the summits rarely take more than one or two hours. Yet in spite of these advantages, climbing in Norway is still in its infancy, with large areas relatively unexplored, and the scope for new climbs seems limitless.

Most of the early development in Romsdal was the work of Arne Randers Heen and other Norwegian climbers, and the great classic route is the Trollryggen East Pillar, climbed by Arne and Ralph Høibakk in 1958, but it was the first ascent of the Trolltind Wall in 1965, one of the highest vertical rock walls in Europe, that really drew the attention of leading British and Continental climbers to this climbing Mecca. This first ascent, by Tony Howard and his companions, must rank as one of the greatest ever achievements by British rock climbers.

It is due to Tony's continuing enthusiasm and hard work that we can all now benefit from this comprehensive guide.

Romsdal
Yves Boussard, 1970

S'il est un paradis du grimpeur, c'est certainement le Massif du Romsdal. Voilà une affirmation bien catégorique, et qui demande des explications.

Quelles qualités doivent réunir un centre d'escalade pour pouvoir prétendre à ce titre? Eh bien, des qualités tres diverses. D'abord, être accessible à tous, du modeste débutant au super-spécialiste:le Romsdal présente un éventail de possibilités capable de satisfaire celui-ci-tout autant que celui-là (et quand je dis 'satisfaire'. certains risquent même de voir leurs espérances quelque peu dépassées) De longues escalades faciles conduisent à de magnifiques sommets par des voies parfois trés aériennes. De très longues traversées sont également possibles d'un sommet à l'autre, par des arêtes très découpées, comme l'arête des Trolls. Les grimpeurs moyens, ou ayant dépassé l'âge des fantaisies, y trouveront également leur bonheur: de nombreux itinéraires AD ou D les conduiront en toute sécurité aux plus beaux sommets de la région. Les bons grimpeurs pourront, entre autres escalades, gravir l'arête Est du Trollryggen – magnifique arête de 1,600 mètres, partant pratiquement de la vallée. (Record de 12 heures des premiers ascensionnistes reste invaincu malgré plusieurs répétitions.) Quant aux spécialistes, si ce sont des habitués de Chamonix, ils n'auront pas lieu de regretter leur Dru ou leurs Aiguilles,car tant du point de vue de la longeur que de la difficulté, le Romsdal leur offrira l équivalent et souvent mieux, dans un rocher excellent, moins compact que la protogyne chamoniarde mais permettant une escalade

Midnight over the Romsdal mountains

plus variée. Les Dolomitars ne seront pas décus non plus. Ils retrouveront au Romsdal les mêmes voies surplombantes avec le même 'gaz' impressionnant, les mêmes relais sur étriers, bivoacs sur escarpolettes et autres petites douceurs. L'escalade sera sans doute un peu plus athlétique, peut-être aussi un peu plus artificiel, (est-ce un mal?) Quant à l'envergure, trouve-t-on dans les Dolomites beaucoup de voies de 1,000 ou 1,200 mètres, presqu'entièrement verticales ou surplombantes? Chamoniards ou Dolomitars pourront escalader, par exemple – s'ils sont bien entraînés – la voie britannique de la Face Nord du Trollryggen, escalade de deux ou trois jours, qui a été comparée par les grimpeurs de l'Androsace à la face ouest des petites Jorasses pour le libre, et à celle du Dru pour l'artificiel. Et, s'ils ont du temps et du matériel, pourquoi n'essaieraient-ils pas la voie française à cette même Face Nord? De l'avis de Dolomitars avertis, cette voie n'a pas son équivalent en Europe: aucune ne présente de tels surplombs, aucune n'a cette continuité dans les difficultés. N'y a-t-il pas là de quoi tenter les plus exigeants?

Autre qualité requise: un climat favorable. A quoi sert d'avoir de belles montagnes, si le temps ne permet pas de mettre le nez dehors? Le climat norvégien est pendant l'été doux et humide. La pluie n'y est pas rare, mais c'est le plus souvent une bruine comparable à la bruine bretonne et qui ne s'oppose pas réellement à l'escalade, car le rocher très rugueux garde une bonne adhérence, même très humide. Mais que l'on ne croie surtout pas que le soleil est absent de Norvège; il s'y montre, et même longremps en été – ou la nuit est pratiquement inexistante ou en tous cas très courte (trois heures fin Juillet). C'est un climat très agréable et très sain (pas un seul d'entre nous, lors de notre expédition de 1967, n'a attrapé le moindre rhume). Mais, dirons les 'purs Alpinistes', ce n'est pas de la montagne! Un climat de bord de mer, pas de neige, ce n'est pas serieux! Rassurons-les vite. Il arrive aussi que le temps se gâte et qu'il neige en altitude. On s'apercoit alors qu'il n'est guère plus confortable d'être bloqué par le mauvais temps dans une voie du Romsdal que dans la Face Ouest des Drus. Toutefois, de grosses chutes de neige ne sont pas à craindre avant le mois de Septembre. Et on peut être certain, en un mois de norvège, de faire près d'un mois d'escalade – je connais certains endroits dont on ne pourrait dire autant.

ll faut, enfin, une 'ambiance': est-ce que ça sent l'escalade à Åndalsnes, le vent des premières y souffle-t-il? Certes, oui, il y souffle, et même fort. Il ne se passe pas une journée d'été sans qu'une nouvelle voie ne soit en cours, et souvent, plusieurs à la fois. Les journaux locaux ont fort à faire, et ce n'est qu'un début. Un nombre infini de premières reste à faire dans le Massif du Romsdal et de toutes difficultés. Tout cela n'est-il pas suffisant pour qualifier le Romsdal de paradis du grimpeur?

Mais il n'y a pas que cela. Il y a ce dépaysement, propre aux Pays du Nord, ces nuits si courtes qui transforment le bivouac en un relai un peu plus prolongé que les autres. Disparue, cette hantise de l'horaire: ne pas être pris par la nuit. Ici, cela n'a pas d'importance: on attend deux ou trois heures, et puis on repart, on dormira dans la vallée. Il y a aussi le paysage, la forêt et les prairies si vertes, les torrents si bleus d'un bleu iréel, transparent, où l'on voit parfois sauter de gros saumons, la petite ville d'Åndalsnes, et ses habitants très hospitaliers, et le port d' Ålesund, que l'on découvre en sortant de l'avion, avec son air de port breton et ses hordes de mouettes criardes. On a peine à croire, alors, qu à quelque distance de là se trouvent des parois parmi les plus belles d'Europe. C'est à tout cela, et à bien d' autres choses encore, que vous invite l'alpiniste norvégien Ralph Høibakk: 'Venez en Norvège, vous y entendrez chanter les pitons de minuit'.

Renseignements d'ordre pratique
– Le voyage peut se faire en avion de Paris, en six heures environ, à Ålesund / Molde. Ensuite un bac, puis un autocar conduisent à Åndalsnes.

– On peut s'y rendre plus économiquement en trois ou quatre jours en voiture. Celle-ci doit être robuste, car les routes ne sont pas excellentes. Ce voyage est très concevable par des grimpeurs ne disposant que d'un mois de vacances.

– La vie en Norvége est coûteuse qu'en France.

– La plupart des Norvégiens parlent anglais.

Author's Acknowledgements

1970 edition. Without the generous help and advice of numerous friends, Norwegian and British, this guide book could hardly have achieved the detailed coverage which has been attempted. In particular I am indebted to many climbers for making available details of their routes, and to B Tweedale for his assistance in collecting the various notes together. I am also grateful to Joe Brown and Yves Boussard for introducing the subject to a European readership.

Arne Heen, Norway's veteran mountain guide, has supplied an expert historical background and Børre Grønningsaeter has written the section on Geology, Flora and Fauna. Both contributions have added extra interest to the book and I deeply appreciate them. My thanks are also due to Halvor Sødahl and his parents at Åndalsnes Foto who have supplied most of the photographs, and who, with Odd Meringdal, the Tourist Director of the region, have given practical help and encouragement. The following Åndalsnes firms all contributed in some measure to the completed manuscript and to them also, my thanks are due: : Brødr. Nedregaard, Matsenteret; Vangen Handel; P R Berge and Astrid; Romsdal Bokhandel; Åndalsnes Avis and Romsdal Budstikke; P Mjelva; Rauma Kafe and Pensjonat; Asbjorn Berger; Bergens Privatbank.

Finally, although I have attempted to make this volume as complete as possible at the time of going to press, Romsdal is a developing area and new climbs can be expected each season. For the benefit of future editions it would be appreciated if any climbers or walkers having useful comments to make on routes in this book, would send the details to the author.

1979 edition. Since writing the above In 1970, exploration of new routes in the area by British climbers has been minimal. The main deterrent has probably been the extraordinary rise in the cost of living in Norway (and travelling there). However new routes and comments on existing routes have been included to bring the book once more up to date. For the notes on these routes, I must thank in particular Hans Christian Doseth of Åndalsnes – a brilliant young climber and a great character who has added some magnificent summer and winter climbs since the publication of the first edition.

2005 edition. It is now around 37 years since I was climbing every year in Romsdal so it has been a real pleasure for me to return to 'The Valley' in recent years and to be welcomed as always by friends old and new. I would especially like to thank my old friend Halvor Sødahl and family of Åndalsnes Foto, not just for providing photos for every edition of this guide, but for remaining a true friend and a crazy Viking! His daughter, Heidi Beate Linneweh, has also been of particular assistance helping with photos and local information and put me in touch with Thomas Brekken, Manager of Åndalsnes and Romsdal Travel Association, who likewise helped considerably with the latest information and sourcing photos. Geir Kleopaker and Bernd Linneweh, both of Åndalsnes Foto, have also provided pictures. For other photos I am indebted to the following whose contributions have added so much to the interest and quality of this edition: Iver Gjelstenli, Øyvind Heen, Fred Husøy, Lars Rikard Morstøl, Kyrre Østbø, Bjorn Rikard Morstøl, E Birkeland and also Di Taylor.

With regard to old friends, it was also great to see Per Harvold again with whom we climbed the Trollryggen Pillar back in the 1960s; also Per Midtgaard who was brave enough to let us build the log cabins of Moen Motel (now Trollstigen Hytteutleie) when we were short of money to support our climbing addiction! I was also very pleased to be able to meet Herbert Gruner again a few years ago – he was one of the great 'old timers' of the mountains, and has since sadly passed away, as has Arne Randers Heen who was a legend in his own time. (Arne's wife Bodil keeps a museum to his memory with artefacts from his early climbs.) Tragically, Hans Christian Doseth, that other great Romsdal activist, met his death on the Trango Tower in Pakistan in 1984 and is also a great loss to the Romsdal scene. Equally sadly, my old climbing partners on many great first ascents in Romsdal and elsewhere, Bill Tweedale and Wayne Gartside, also recently passed away.

On a happier note, it was very good to meet the new generation of Romsdal climbers, such as Terje Ormseth Olsen, Halvor Hagen and Kyrre Østbø who organised our visit to the 2003 Romsdal Fjell Festival. Both Halvor Hagen and Bjarte Bø have done the Rimmon Route on the Troll Wall in less than 8 hours as well as making their own new climbs on walls both big and small. Iver Gjelstenli is another Romsdal climber who took over where we left off – strangely, we met him a few years ago in Wadi Rum, Jordan, another of our 'happy hunting grounds'. Finally, Fred Husøy of Aak is an old friend and has been of particular assistance in helping to make sure that the updated information in this edition is correct. Thanks a lot, Fred, and thanks also to Bjarte for permission to use some details from *Klatring i Romsdal*.

Back in the UK, Wendy Hughes of the Norwegian Tourist Board has been of great help, whilst Dave Cummins and Suzanne Troop of The Bank Creative Consultancy gave their time and expertise to make the third and fourth editions possible. I should also thank Cicerone Press for support of earlier editions and Cordee for their work on this one. Also, I mustn't forget to thank Di Taylor, my partner both on and off the mountains not only for her infectious enthusiasm for exploring the world's mountains, but also for giving me the inspiration to complete this book and for doing so much work towards it!

Tony Howard, www.nomadstravel.co.uk, 2004

Introduction

The purpose of this book is to provide not simply the necessary practical information that climbers would expect but also some descriptive interest so that readers can 'see' and enjoy Romsdal and its rare delights for themselves, whether they happen to be sitting comfortably at home or curled up in a bivouac in the mountains. Hopefully, in doing so, they will be able to savour the pleasure of anticipation for here indeed is 'a place where every prospect pleases and variety is infinite'.

Norway in the 1960s was probably the only country in Europe where mountain exploration was hardly beyond its infancy. Yet, to quote from Per Prag in his 1963 guide *Mountain Holidays in Norway*, 'few tourist districts in Norway have evoked more lyrical outbursts than Romsdal, the valley with its mountain ranges is said to be a worthy rival to the Yosemite itself, and the Romsdalshorn has been compared with the Matterhorn. The scenery is fascinating and the whole district is ideal for walking tours and rock climbs'.

Small wonder then that Romsdal has at last come into the limelight of mountaineering, for here indeed are rock faces the equal of any in the Alps, with routes of all grades of difficulty, some as hard as any in Europe. Many rise almost from sea level to 2,000m, are easy to approach and stand in settings of beauty that for years have been unknown to the vast majority of mountaineers in Britain and in Europe as a whole.

Not surprisingly most of the attention has been attracted to difficult routes on great vertical walls such as the 1,200m Troll Wall or to the immense ridges such as the mile-long Trollryggen Pillar. There are in fact many quite wonderful routes that are rarely above Grade III and are highly popular amongst the Norwegians. The merest glance at the Graded List of Walks, Scrambles and Climbs shows what a marvellous selection of these easier excursions is to be found.

Most of the traditional routes were first described in the *Mountain Holidays* guide published by the Norwegian National Tourist Office. This excellent little book contains a wealth of general information but gives few exact details of the climbs in each area. Since its publication mountaineering in Romsdal has developed phenomenally. Of the routes described here about 25 per cent are ascents first made since 1962. The French Direct Route on Trollveggen (The Troll Wall), one of the most difficult climbs, required the use of 600 pegs and almost a mile of rope – a far cry from the ascent of the Romsdalshorn in 1827 by two local farmers after 'a dare during a merry drinking party'! Hans Bjermeland and Christian Hoel had reached the summit by 'alternately pushing and pulling' and built a massive cairn which still stands.

This book describes the best known walks and climbs that have been made since that early ascent of Norway's most famous mountain. It is the first book to describe in detail an entire mountain area of Norway, Romsdal being the first region to have developed to an extent meriting publication of an independent guide. The other areas are relatively unknown to all but a few mountaineers, mostly Norwegian, but are well worth visiting. From Lyngen and Lofoten to the Jostedal and Jotunheim and the superb Setesdal Slabs and sea cliffs of the south it is a fascinating midnight sun world of remote and beautiful mountains in the legendary home of the Trolls. Romsdal itself is an area of wonderful peaks of snow and rock, of high lonely glaciers and tremendous glaciated walls, of deep birch-clad valleys and roaring waterfalls and, more than anything, of solitude. Here is true mountaineering amidst the grandeur of peaks in virgin aloofness above idyllic valleys. Amongst them it is still rare to meet another person.

2003. Since the 1970s, the Troll Wall has become intertwined with routes (some of which, including The Rimmon and Swedish Routes, have been seriously damaged by giant rock falls).

Other more hospitable cliffs such as Klauva, Mjølva, Hornaksla and Norafjell have yielded many excellent new climbs. Delightful bouldering areas have also been developed. Even so, many obvious lines still remain both on the big walls and smaller cliffs. Indeed, away from the most popular walks and climbs you are still likely to have the mountains pretty much to yourself – an increasingly precious experience not to be missed.

Åndalsnes, The Alpine Village by the Fjord
Odd Meringdal, Tourist Director, 1970.

The huge ice glaciers that once covered our west coast were nature's architects of the beautiful and spectacular valleys and mountains, lakes and fjords of Norway. A few English mountaineers and salmon fishermen first discovered the area over a hundred and twenty years ago and no region was given greater acclaim than Romsdal.

The inner parts of Romsdal present a majestic panorama which, for size, variety and beauty has to be seen to be believed. Mountains rise 2,000m sheer from the dales and lakes. Those facing the Atlantic Ocean have the images of savage giants and the superstitious of long ago named them the Trolls, the fearsome beings of Scandinavian mythology. Many of our peaks in the area are prefixed with Troll names. The best known is perhaps the mighty Trollveggen, the Troll Wall, ascents of which are described in this book. Its vertical precipice of over 1,200m is the highest in Europe.

The country area is lightly populated having only about five persons per square kilometre. Farming is the main occupation though only four to five per cent of the area is under cultivation. Salmon and trout abound, and in the mountains game and wild reindeer are numerous. It is a region of beautiful waterfalls, some harnessed to provide cheap electricity, others preserved as natural attractions. The thundering Mardalsfoss is Europe's greatest waterfall. Set amidst it all at the foot of the mountains is the tourist and traffic centre of Åndalsnes by the shores of the

View of Åndalsnes and Romsdal from Trolltind Massif

Geir 2001

Romsdalsfjord – 'The Alpine Village by the Fjord'. Each year, and regularly increasing, a quarter of a million tourists come during the summer season. There are about 1,000 beds in hotels, pensions, motels and camping huts and every year more are being provided. Some 20 tourist-liners bring approximately 9,000 visitors up the fjord to call at the famous little town. Most of them take the coach trip to Trollstigen, 780m above sea level, a breathtaking journey up one of the most famed roads of Europe. It snakes up the face of the almost vertical mountainside in eleven tight hairpin bends and passes through the spray of the beautiful Stigfoss waterfall.

There is an extensive choice of day trips in the area – to Lake Eikesdal, one of the loveliest of Norway's mountain lakes, to Kristiansund, a many-coloured town by the sea, to Ålesund with its old fishing wharf, to Geiranger, one of our most attractive fjords, and many other beauty spots.

Åndalsnes is easy to reach from Oslo, being at the end of the Raumabanen, the railroad from the capital. In Romsdal there are many excellent camping places. And yet, for all the growing popularity of the area, up in the mountains it is still unusual to see other people. Perhaps, for mountaineers, we are the first and last haven In Europe for those who still seek that serenity of perfect peace and quiet which only mountains can afford. Velkommen til Åndalsnes.

Geology, Flora and Fauna
Børre I Grønningsaeter

For many years the mountains of Romsdal have been admired with wonder and interest by the tourists and local mountain people whose imaginations were captured by their size and shapes, but who knew little of their origin and formation.

A little geological research can tell us a great deal about this mountain region. The greatest part of the present mountains in west Norway were formed about 5–600 million years ago by the sedimentation of sand and mud in an extremely deep sea basin, due to the erosion of even older rocks. These deposits, many thousands of feet in thickness, became under great pressure, rocks which eventually rose to form a new coastline. About 300 million years ago, movement and folding completed their formation and signs of this folding action are visible in many places around Romsdal. The great fold which follows the whole of the Norwegian coast is known as 'the Caledonian earth-crust fold'. It is, of course named after Caledonia, the old name for Scotland where this fold was first found.

Because of this origin, most of the rocks of west Norway, including those of Romsdal are of quartz, fellspar and mica, these being the basis of the gneiss and granite of which the mountains are formed. Much of the rock is, in fact, gneiss and the colour varies from quite light to almost black depending upon the varying amounts of quartz, fellspar and mica involved in its formation. The quartz and fellspar are white or light coloured, the mica is mostly black but can be light or silver-white. The dark is called biotite mica, the light, muscovite, and dependent upon which form this takes, we get biotite or muscovite gneiss and granite. In the Romsdal mountains, the dark biotite is the most common though the rock can be quite light if the fellspar or quartz is dominant. The fellspar and quartz often occur in broad bands. One such goes from the foot of Bispen, across Trollstigen to Stighorn, crossing the track to the Stigfoss viewpoint where it is very obvious. In this band is a great deal of muscovite mica. The end of another band is marked by the 'yellow fleck' on Romsdalshorn.

The climate in the high mountains can be very cold, often with rain and snow, eroding the mountains in the summer and splitting rocks with the help of ice in the winter. These actions have played a great part in the formation of the mountains just as, in the past, the giant glaciers of the ice age carved out the valleys and fjords of Romsdal and the whole of Norway.

Vengetind from Romsdal

Only 10–12,000 years ago the country was covered in ice. Many biologists think that the highest tops such as Vengetind, Trolltind and Finnan in Romsdal were visible, even when the ice was at its thickest. They also think that there may have been an ice-free zone along the coast, but glaciologists and geologists disagree with this theory. They propose that even the highest peaks were covered by a thick layer of ice that not only covered the coast line but extended as far as the Faroe Islands. The movement of this ice inevitably polished the rocks forming the glacier bed and gorged out deep valleys. Furthermore the 2,000m thick ice cap was so enormous that the land beneath sunk beneath its weight or was pushed aside. At the weakest points extremely deep valleys were formed – today's dales and fjords

Eventually when the mountains were free of ice, the land lifted again and so far it has risen about 120m. The land on which Sogge Farm is now situated, beneath the Trolltinder, was at one time under the sea, and like most of the valleys in Romsdal was the inner end of the fjord-system. The deposits carried down into the fjords from the mountains have risen and formed good land for agricultural purposes.

Today there are few glaciers left in Romsdal but some remain high in the mountains, for instance on Vengetind, Kvandalstind, Trolltind and Finnan. The Finnan Glacier, near Trollstig has been studied by the Norsk Polar Institute for 20 years and has been shown to have receded every year. In recent years the summers have been warmer and the whole of the glacier area is diminishing more quickly, as is the case with other glaciers throughout Norway. (By 2003, this process had visibly accelerated, causing rock falls such as those on Trollveggen and melting the snowfields usually found below Trollveggen. Snow normally found on the tops of most of Romsdal's high summits throughout the year had also almost gone in the summer of 2003. *Author.*)

In the mountains of Romsdal, and other parts of Norway, there are often areas where there is little vegetation. These are places where the ice has only just retreated and the vegetation is not yet established, leaving clear rock. By studying the areas around the tongues of the glaciers it is easy to discover the type of plant that first established themselves. After many years of observation it has been noted that amongst the first to grow is a small mountain grass called Fjellrap (*Poa Alpina*). It is followed by *Rununculus Glacialis* and *Oxyria Digyna*. Later, came *Saxifrage Stellaris* and other plants. This latter is one of Norway's most best known little mountain flowers: it is called Fjell Dronninga – The Mountain Queen and grows all over west Norway from the fjords to the high mountains. Many are found on Bispen and Kongen in Isterdal even above 1,500m, which is the highest they are known to grow in the whole of Norway. (Not far away to the south east of Romsdal and just north of Dombås on the road from Oslo, is Dovrefjell National Park. At the Kongsvoll Fjeldstua access point, there is an area of wild hillside rich in plant life with pathways amongst the labelled flora. Inside the park itself, on the approach to the Reinheim Hut and Snøhetta (2,200m) walkers will also find the mighty muskox, a small herd of them having been brought from Greenland almost 100 years ago and now flourishing. *Author, 2003*).

There is also much wild life in the Romsdal mountains, as elsewhere in Norway, though the bears which used to roam these mountains are now extinct. This is, of course, something the local farmers are happy about as in the late 1980s, their livestock was in jeopardy from these animals. Nowadays their main worry is the lynx, which is still fairly common. There are many herds of reindeer and there are also ptarmigan, hares and foxes. Even the eagle can still be found in its mountain eyrie, defying the hunter and challenged only by the climber!

Historical (to 1970)
Arne Randers Heen

The first ascent of any large peak in the north of Europe occurred in 1827 on the Romsdalshorn which rises near Åndalsnes. Two peasants, Christen Hoel and Hans Bjermeland, succeeded in reaching the top and built a cairn there. That was in an age when climbing was almost unknown. Even the mountains scaled in the Alps at that time were chiefly mere stamping in snow. Later, many foreign tourists visited the Romsdal valley. Some tried to reach the Horn, but in vain. About 1860 an Englishman, Bromley-Davenport, bought a farm with a salmon river at the foot of the Trolltinder and, in 1870 probably, made the first ascent of Nordre Trolltind with J Venge, a local man.

The climber who did most to open the mountains in Norway was a Dane, Carl Hall, who wrote many articles for the annual editions of *Norske Turistforening*. In 1881 he gained Romsdalshorn on his seventh attempt accompanied by two local guides M Soggemoen and E Norahagen. In the following years Hall was the leader on the first ascent of Store Trolltind in 1885, Bispen, Kongen and Dronninga in 1892, Hoemstind in 1893 and Finnan in 1898.

Near the foot of the Horn at Aak is a farm where the owner began to accept tourists in about 1860. A great many of them were English. Some wrote books which made Romsdal better known. Amongst these was a young girl, Lady Di Beauclerk who, in 1868, in her charming book *A Summer and Winter in Norway*, tells about the days at Aak (now Hotel Aak) as 'a stay in heaven'. The well known English climber W C Slingsby first visited Aak in 1875. In 1881, with a Norwegian partner, he made the first ascent of Store Vengetind and later Lille Vengetind in 1884, and Kvandalstind in 1885. He regarded Kvandalstind as 'the steepest mountain in Europe'. In 1903 he wrote *Norway, the Northern Playground*, the first book about mountaineering in Norway and still worth reading. It opened up the country for the English-speaking world and was republished by Ripping Yarns in 2003.

Carl Hall, Eric Norahagen and Mathias Soggemoen, 1881

In 1893 the Englishmen Patchell and Bowen ascended the South East Ridge of Kvandalstind which they called 'the finest rock climb in Europe'. W Napier with Norahagen was on Juratind in 1884 and wrote about its 'first ascent', but it had been climbed previously in 1880 by two shepherd boys.

The old guides always led the visitors to the peaks by the easiest way and there was rarely any question of climbing as a sport in itself. Gradually however climbers found their way to Romsdal, and some of the inhabitants began to show interest in seeking new routes. In 1908 the Norwegian Alpine Club was founded with members chiefly from Oslo. The

North Wall of Romsdalshorn and the West Ridge of Kvandalstind were climbed in 1920. Next came more difficult routes such as the Romsdalshorn West Wall in 1928, then in 1929, the South Wall and in 1947 the East Arête. On Vengetind in 1930 the West Ridge was climbed and in 1935 the South wall. On Trolltind in 1927 the ascent of its North Ridge was made, followed by the Fiva Route on its east side in 1931. In 1939 Dronninga's east side was climbed.

These two latter climbs were the first of the big face routes and the question then arose whether any part of the east or north ramparts of Trollryggen were possible. The most prominent line leads up the East Pillar of Trollryggen and was climbed in 1958 by A Randers Heen and R Høibakk. This was the first climb in the area where it was necessary to bivouac on the route. An article about this route, with photos, was published in European mountaineering magazines, and then came the question of the Troll Wall itself. That would be climbing of the highest standard in comparison with any routes that had been made in the Alps.

Climbers from several nations arrived in Åndalsnes to solve this problem and on the same day in 1965, a Norwegian and an English party started on the Wall. The Norwegians chose a long route on the left side and the English took the entrance higher up on the slabs. Artificial equipment had to be used and after about two weeks both parties reached the top. The Direct Route between these two routes was still waiting, and in 1967 a French party engaged on it. It was the greatest climbing problem in the north of Europe if not the whole of Europe, and was given much publicity in the press. By much artificial aid and excellent organisation they gained the summit after three weeks of concentrated and sustained effort. On the same day an Anglo-Norwegian party conquered the overhanging East Wall on Kongen and, shortly after, two English climbers made the North Wall of Søndre Trolltind by much artificial work, though without the siege tactics adopted by the French.

Meanwhile, famous British climbers Joe Brown and Tom Patey were busy opening up routes such as the 1,500m North West Rib of Goksøyra and the even longer South East Ridge of Nordre Trolltind. Tony Howard, Bill Tweedale, Rob Holt and Wayne Gartside, all members of a newly formed Romsdal Guides Corps also made many other classic first ascents throughout the season beginning in late winter whilst there was still much snow, with the South West Pillar of Holstind. Next, they climbed the South East face of Kongen, and then two of Romsdal's famous 'Three Pillars', the East Pillar of Breitind and the East Pillar of Søndre Trolltind. At the same time they also found their services as guides to be in increasing demand from new visitors and tourists, also climbers from Britain and most of the European countries.

In 1968, Tony Howard and Bill Tweedale made Norwegian climbing history by leading a client (Per Harvold of Åndalsnes) up the Trollryggen Pillar. This route also had its first female ascent that season – by two Polish girls, Halina Kruger and Wanda Rutkiewicz. A R Heen and R Høibakk made their jubilee ascent and the tenth ascent of the route in a record time of 14 hours.

Elsewhere in 1968, the Guides made first ascents on Kvandalstind, Stighorn and Finnan. The East Face of Goksøyra succumbed to a Norwegian team and the East Pillar of Brudgommen to a Polish team. The hardest route of the season – Mongejura's West Diedre fell to a British team. The still unclimbed (and by then almost legendary) Høibakk's Chimneys on Søndre Trolltind rebuffed all attempts for the fourth year in succession.

Next season – the summer of 1969 – they were to capitulate to a British party, but not without artificial aid. Also that season, another British team including Tony Wilmott made the first ascents of two long routes on Romsdalshorn and Søndre Trolltind. Two other well known climbers, also from England – Ed Ward Drummond and Dave Pearce, made a superb attempt at the French Route in a single push. Using 'Yosemite Techniques' they reached a point below the main roofs in only four days. Unfortunately a false line and lack of water forced retreat onto the East Pillar.

By this time, the climbing season had grown considerably, with climbing teams present both summer and winter. Historically the first winter climb was on Romsdalshorn in March 1930 by A R Heen and O Ashaug. This peak is now being climbed all the year round. In fact, by 1932 almost all the peaks in the Romsdal area had been ascended in wintertime.

Because most of the pioneer climbers who reached the various summits wrote their names in the guide's personal record books or in the guest book at Aak, Arne Randers Heen was able to record them all in 'Summit Books' safely secured in boxes placed by the cairns on the tops of the peaks. They are a record of Romsdal's mountaineering history and their pages now await the signatures of all the many who will follow as the rare attractions of the region become ever more widely known.

Historical (from 1970)
Tony Howard

During the 1970s, when I went off to the Yukon, North Africa and elsewhere, exploration of Romsdal's mountains had a much more local emphasis. Young climbers such as Hans Doseth, K Svanemyr and B Østigard were the leading lights, opening up numerous high quality hard new climbs on both big walls and small crags such as Blånebba, Goksøyra, Hornaksla, Norafjell, Mjelva and the newly discovered but excellent cliff of Klauva above Isfjord. They also discovered Romsdal's superb ice-fall climbing. However, they did not have it all to themselves. In 1970, Doug Scott and friends opened two new climbs on Adelsfjell whilst Ben Campbell-Kelly and A Ferguson added two on Setnesfjell. Then, in the winter of 1972, Ed Ward Drummond and H Drummond climbed their epic Arch Wall on the Troll Wall. In 1975, Cathcart and Slaney added their East Face Route on Store Trolltind. Also during the '70s, Polish climbers were extremely active in winter, making ascents of Breitind's East Pillar and South East Ridge (1974 and '76) and the East Pillar of Søndre Trolltind and the East Face of Hornaksla, both in 1974. On the Troll Wall they made winter ascents of the French Route in 1974 and the Rimmon Route in 1976, whilst Steve Bancroft, Choe Brooks and Hans Doseth climbed the Swedish Route free in 1980.

Geiranger Fjord on 'The Golden Route' to Romsdal

After then, the vast majority of new routes have been done by Romsdal climbers and other Norwegians. Some are on newly discovered small cliffs and boulders as befits today's trends, others are on the traditional 'big walls'. They are predominantly (though not always) in the higher grades (6 and upwards) and are described in *Klatring in Romsdal* – see the section 'Maps, Guides and Info on Norway'.

Travel

There are various ways of travelling from Britain to Åndalsnes. By air and road the journey takes about 12 hours, whilst by sea and road (or rail) it takes about two days.

Getting there:

Fjord Line: For sailings from Newcastle to Stavanger, Haugesund and Bergen in western Norway, and info on motoring and cottage holidays. Tel: 0191 296 1313, website: www.fjordline.co.uk

If you are driving up from Bergen, the best route is via Voss, Balestrand, Loen, Stryn, Grotli, Geiranger and Trollstigen. This is 'The Golden Route', a great scenic drive of about 500km for which you should allow two days at least, to enjoy it. You could also stop off in the Jotunheim, Norway's highest mountains en route. Mountain passes open officially on 5 June, but always check first.

DFDS Seaways: For sailings from Newcastle to Kristiansund in south Norway, and self-drive holidays. Tel: 0870 848 8222, website: www.dfds.seaways.co.uk

Though it's a long drive up to Romsdal from Kristiansund, the route passes through the beautiful valley of Setesdal where there are some excellent 300m slab climbs and steeper walls before you have the option of picking up the E136 from Oslo or visiting the snow capped mountains of the eastern Jotunheim.

SAS – Scandinavian Airlines: For daily flights from the UK to Oslo, Bergen and Stavanger, as well as domestic flights within Norway. Tel: 0845 607 2772, website: www.scandinavian.net

Ryanair: Ryanair operate a service from London Stansted and Glasgow Prestwick to Oslo (south) Torp airport approximately 130km from Oslo. In addition they operate a service between Stansted and Haugesund, which is south of Bergen, and are planning a service to Ålesund at the entrance to Romsdalsfjord. Website: www.ryanair.co.uk

Norwegian Air Shuttle: This privately owned budget carrier is to introduce a four times weekly non-stop service from Stansted to Trondheim, north of Romsdal. They have also introduced services from Stansted to Bergen, Oslo and Stavangar. See: www.norwegian.no

Coming overland from the continent, there is a direct ferry from Copenhagen to Oslo (by night). In addition there are ferrys from Frederikshavn to both Kristiansund and Larvik. Color Line also have a direct ferry from Kiel (Germany) to Oslo that is much used by Norwegians on their way to/from the continent. For routes and prices see: www.dfds.com and www.colorline.no

Getting around:

Norwegian State Railways: Established in 1854, NSB is still one of Norway's most important transport companies: the comfortable and relaxing way of experiencing Norway. Website: www.nsb.no

Ferries: Ferries and express boats are a pleasant and almost essential part of the transport system in and to the Romsdal area. Website: www.mrf.no

Bus/Coach Travel: You will find you can get practically anywhere you want to in Norway by bus. Usually it is not necessary to pre-book, you simply pay the driver on boarding the bus. See: NOR-WAY Bus Express. Tel: 00 47 815 44 444, website: www.nor-way.no

Hiring a Car: Most of the major car hire companies are able to arrange transportation in Norway.

Avis: 0870 6060 100. Budget: 0800 181 1181. Hertz: 08705 996 699

Public transport facilities in Romsdal are adequate, there being bus services up all the valleys. A small sum is sufficient to travel to any of the starting points in the central massif. For those with their own cars, fuel prices compare with Britain. Most roads are excellent though the small, older roads are mostly made of water bound gravel. This is hardly surprising as they are covered with snow for about five months in the year! Some of the roads into the high mountain valleys such as Vengedal are private toll roads, a small fee being payable at the 'honesty box' usually marked 'Bom'. The Trollstig Pass between Åndalsnes and Valldal is usually opened by the end of May, but this depends on the snow conditions.

There are a number of garages in Åndalsnes with good service and repair facilities.

Amenities and Guiding Services

Åndalsnes is well served by shops and stores but most goods in Norway are considerably more expensive than in the UK. Outdoor wear, sportswear and clothing of Norwegian design and manufacture are all available, as is equipment for skiing, camping and fishing. There is an excellent bookshop called Romsdal Libris (just down the street from the post office) with books in most languages and guidebooks and maps to the area. There are also two good photographic equipment stockists, Åndalsnes Foto, owned by our good friend Halvor Sødahl being just right of the book shop.

Almost all foodstuffs are available in Åndalsnes though imported goods tend to be expensive. Fish, of course, is fresh and reasonably priced as are milk and eggs. Fruit, vegetables and bread are not too expensive, likewise some dehydrated foods. There are many varieties of cheese, some quite cheap, but jam and preserves are on the dear side. For eating out, there are numerous coffee bars, ice cream and pizza parlours and cafés. Again, prices seem at first glance to be expensive but with judicious buying of soups, *lapskaus* and similar 'meals of the day' a reasonably priced and good meal can be had. Unlike the 'prohibition' days of the '60s, there are now pubs in town, but alcoholic drinks are definitely dear, even in the supermarkets.

There are a number of resident mountain guides in Romsdal. For information about guide services see www.norgesguidene.no and www.tinderogbanditter.com.

An excellent website with lots of information about Åndalsnes and Romsdal, amenities, festivals, accommodation, camping, hiking, climbing and guiding is www.visitandalsnes.com.

Another very good site with a lot of information about Romsdal and its mountains is www.romsdalsalpene.com.

All these websites have links to activities, culture and accommodation. Anyone needing on-site information should enquire at the tourist information office in the station.

Entertainment

Apart from the few pubs, there is also a cinema in Åndalsnes with a good selection of films, often British or American, and subtitled in Norwegian. There is also a swimming pool with showers and sauna (separate days for men and women). Below the Grand Hotel, the Buona Notte disco is open three nights a week and there are sometimes Saturday night dances with music by local pop or folk groups. Nearby villages such as Isfjord, Innfjord, Måndal, or Bjorli also have occasional Saturday evening dances.

Amongst the festive annual events celebrated are Norway's National Day (17 May). On the first weekend of June, the Trollstig ski competition is held (snow permitting), then, there is Midsummer's Day. In the next month, during the second week of July, Romsdal holds its Fjell Festival (Mountain Festival) see www.fjellfestivalen.com.

Accommodation

The festival is predominantly an active mountain week, with guided groups making ascents of major summits by scrambles and climbs, as well as enjoying some of Romsdal's many mountain walks. There are also lectures and other events most evenings. Also in July, further down the fjord in Molde, an international jazz festival is held and, in mid August, it's time for Rauma Rock in Åndalsnes (that's rock 'n' roll, not climbing!). Also in August, there is a new annual festival about the 1612 Scottish raid on Romsdal, 'The Sinclair Festival' see: www.sinclairfestivalen.co. Next, in September, Romsdal Martnan, the annual fair, is held.

Those in search of local climbing history will find the Mountain Museum in memory of Arne Randers Heen at the house of Bodil Heen, across the river from Åndalsnes then first left, to the first house along the road.

Accommodation

Accommodation in Romsdal varies from youth hostels, camping and camping huts, pensions and motels to first class hotels. There are pensionats (boarding houses) in all villages. Details are given in the introduction to each area, also see www.visitandalsnes.com.

Some of the most useful for the climber and walker in the central area are:

Hotel Aak (where Slingsby stayed in the 1880s) on the left of the road, coming from Åndalsnes, just before the bridge at the main Romsdal – Isterdal junction.
Tel: 71227171, fax: 71227172, email: hotel@aak.no, website: www.hotelaak.no

Mjelva Camping just 3km from Åndalsnes below Mjølva Cliff.
Tel: 71226450, email: mjelva@eunet.no

Åndalsnes Camping & Motell Tel: 71222279, fax: 71221700,
email: acampi@online.no, website: www.andalsnescamp.no

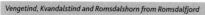
Vengetind, Kvandalstind and Romsdalshorn from Romsdalfjord

Trollveggen Camping almost opposite the Troll Wall and near Hornaksla.
Tel: 71223700, fax: 71221631

Soggebru Camping, at the entrance to Isterdal. Tel: 712214 82

Trollstigen Hytteutleie & Camping, up the road to Isterdal from Sogge.
Tel: 71226899, email: kirst-kj@online.no

Trollstigen Camping in Isterdal, with views to Bispen, Kongen and Dronninga,
Tel: 71221112, fax: 71222248, email: ed-mey@online.no, website: www.trollcamp.no

Campsite prices are not unreasonable and full facilities are generally available, with hut accommodation should you prefer it. Wild camping is permitted almost anywhere for a couple of nights without charge, though there are very few wild places down in the valley. If you do find a place to camp in the valley, it is polite to enquire first at the nearest farm and to keep well away from homes.

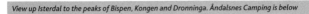

View up Isterdal to the peaks of Bispen, Kongen and Dronninga. Åndalsnes Camping is below

In the main climbing areas, there are no actual mountain huts as in the Alps but, in the popular walking areas on the fringes of Romsdal there are some excellent DNT huts (see the section 'Maps, Guides and Info on Norway' for information on the DNT). All DNT huts are mentioned in the appropriate section and route descriptions of this book. Additionally, across the fjord to the north of Romsdal, in the Isfjord Ranges – a region popular with walkers and fishermen, as well as having some quality climbs – there are some huts owned by the Molde and Romsdal Turistforening. These are Hoemsbu and Måsvassbu (self catering) and Vasstindbu and Svartbu (unstaffed). There is also a hut below Klauva specifically for climbers. All these huts are marked on the Romsdal Turkart and Romsdalsalpene maps, together with the trails. They are open to anyone for a small fee per night, and have from four to eight beds.

Local Attitude

The people are everywhere most hospitable, helpful and friendly. They are proud of their valleys and mountains and pleased to see visitors. These days they are no longer surprised (as they were in the '60s) that anyone should wish to climb a mountain by a difficult route, or indeed climb it at all! Though there is no Norwegian word for 'mountaineering', they make climbers welcome and offer every assistance.

This, as most climbers know, is a rare and much to be prized situation. As Joe Brown said in his Foreword in 1970, there are some parts of Britain and Europe where lack of consideration from both sides led to friction and ill feeling in the 1960s and '70s. As a result campsites were closed, prices rose, and farmers and locals who had hitherto been co-operative began to turn campers and climbers away. Much of this was brought about by carelessness or innocent misunderstanding but there were, nevertheless, climbers who travelled abroad on the 'beg, borrow, or steal' principle. They did a great disservice to the reputation of other climbers amongst the local communities.

The 'climbing-bum' is less evident these days, but nevertheless, such stories reached Romsdal and the writer and his colleagues promised in earlier editions of this book to make an appeal to all who visit this paradise for mountaineers: play fair, treat Romsdal as it will treat you – cheerfully, kindly, and well. It is a simple basic matter of respecting the mountains, the country-side, and the people, your hosts in their country.

Weather

In the summer months on Norway's south and west coasts, the weather is often better for climbing than in the Alps. In early June, providing there is enough of winter's snow remaining, bikini clad skiers often crowd the slopes of Trollstigen, 1,000m up in the mountains, for the the ski championships. Bathing goes on in the Romsdalsfjord and river all through the summer (though I must say I never tried it!).

Not only can the weather be warm – even hot at times – it is probably more predictable than the weather in Britain or other high mountain regions. One of the best guides for local weather conditions is wind direction. If it comes from the sea and the weather is at all dull you can expect it to deteriorate. If it is blowing down the valley and it is a fine day it will almost certainly stay good for some time. Bad weather signs are cloud forming low in the valleys or on the summit of Vengetind.

In this area of Norway there is no real darkness from mid May until the beginning of August. The midnight sun is actually just below the northern horizon for a few hours but it is still usually light enough to climb for 24 hours a day during this period and the traditional early alpine starts are unnecessary. Bivouacking can be a pleasure in its own right. The coldest time is usually about

2am and the light is a bit shadowy from 11pm to 4am. The only snag to a late start is that all the graft (walking) may have to be done in hot sunshine!

Although the peaks are just under 2,000m high, retreat down a route can be extremely long and serious. Bone-dry slabs and walls can become rivers and waterfalls within an hour or so if the weather should break. Thunder and snowstorms are very infrequent but should the latter occur, the summit walls can be plastered with snow and sometimes ice within a very short time. It is well to remember that climbs of 1,500m and over should never be lightly undertaken no matter what their grade may be. For example, on our first ascent of the Søndre Trolltind East Pillar, a 2,000m Grade V, in midsummer, we set off in good weather but were hit by a blizzard and thunder storm below the headwall. Lightning caused a rockfall and Bill Tweedale was hit on the head, splitting his helmet and knocking him unconscious. When he recovered, we climbed on up rock plastered in snow to reach the summit in a white-out. Luckily, with our knowledge of the area, we found the bivouac boulder near Storgrovbotnen, enabling us to descend in better weather the next day, but the changing weather had made what should have been a reasonable route into an epic!

General Equipment

For all walks and most climbs, normal mountain clothing and equipment will be adequate. These days, rock shoes are commonly used on all climbs though 30 or more years ago the routes were done in mountain boots! If you do climb in light smooth soled rock shoes, think carefully about the descents, these often being down gullies and snowfields, so you will need to carry something more substantial.

A single 45m rope is sufficient for all the easier climbs up to Grade III, together with a small rack of medium to large nuts and some slings. On routes above this standard, especially the longer and more serious ones, or routes with abseil descents, most climbers will prefer a double rope of 45m, or better still 50m, thereby enabling long descents to be made by abseil in emergency. However, descents from summits are normally easy even though lengthy and abseils are very rarely necessary except in emergency. The main exception is the Romsdalshorn which not only requires four abseils down the Ordinary Route but, these days, due to its popularity has recently been fitted with five sets of chains by local guides, giving a fast 'abseil piste' down its North Ridge.

Crash helmets are always a sensible precaution though few climbers wear them on the easiest routes. Nevertheless it is these very routes which have the most scree ledges and are therefore the most prone to rock fall if other climbers are above you. The best advice is to wear a crash helmet all the time. It is better to be safe than sorry.

The majority of the climbing is free and any pegs needed on the climbs of Grade III and below are usually for belays and are in place. Not many of the routes above this standard have pegs in situ although a few of the most recent climbs have fixed gear. Unless otherwise stated a dozen pegs and karabiners will be ample for most routes. Only about a dozen of the climbs require pegs for aid and not all of these need the use of etriers. The hardest artificial routes are exceedingly serious undertakings requiring considerable experience and technical knowledge and a large and varied selection of hardware. It is neither usual nor desirable to use siege tactics.

Finally, a cautionary note. Anyone considering an attempt on a route knowing it to be a serious undertaking when measured against their own standard of proficiency should bear in mind this excerpt from a poem by Arne Garborg:

'I've come so oft to desperate grips with Trolldom's power. God help the man whose foothold slips in such an hour'.

Bivouac Equipment

The weather and night climate in the summer months are such that expensive bivouac and down equipment is seldom necessary. On all but the longest multiple-day routes a light bivouac-sack and spare clothing are sufficient. For most routes a spare sweater and waterproof will suffice as a precaution against a change in the weather or the need for an emergency bivouac. In such circumstances climbers should be able to cheerfully survive a day or two on boiled sweets, raisins, and chocolates with bread and cheese for bulk.

As many of the routes are extremely long, speed and hence lightness are prime considerations if aiming to complete the route in a day. Those who cannot contemplate the thought of 12 hours or more without the comfort of a brew will normally find plenty of snow or water. Their handicap of course will be the extra weight of stove and pans.

On routes of three days' duration or longer, warm meals are necessary and dehydrated and concentrated foods should therefore be taken. Unfortunately on all the longest and hardest routes, water can be a problem especially towards the end of the season and it may be necessary to carry a couple of litres per person per day. Bivouac places on all but some of the major climbs are usually palatial, the North Wall of Søndre Trolltind, some of the routes on the Troll Wall and the East Face Direct of Kongen are the only routes where a hammock is necessary.

Snow and Ice

Summer snow and ice climbing is almost non-existent although there are a dozen small glaciers in the area all of which have been climbed. Some, such as Kalskratind's 'Uncharted Glacier', are quite remote and seldom climbed. Others like the Kvandalstind glaciers have easy access and many variations, from easy walks to extreme ice.
For variety and spectacular scenery these are probably the best. The most climbed glacier is however the Nordre Finnan Glacier (above Bispevatnet) at Trollstigen, which has a pleasant climb of 2–4 hours up to the top of Finnan, and with only an hour approach.

Bjørn Bergsvik on 'Porkåla', Verma

All of these are described in this book. Most of the higher peaks have permanent snow couloirs, some over 300m. Many have been climbed and are without difficulty, often providing the fastest routes of descent though with global warming and consequent decreasing snow remaining into the summer, this could change.

The best time of the year for snow and ice climbs is of course winter (November to March) and many technical ice-fall climbs have now been done and are recorded in *Klatring i Romsdal*. Numerous others await first ascents. Some snow routes are also possible in the late season (August to September) when the snow has consolidated in the gullies and the crevasses in the glaciers are visible. In May and early June, the snow is soft and avalanches are numerous. On a

The Troll Wall in winter

warm spring day, the peaks above Romsdal and Isterdal never cease echoing with the thunder of winter's snows descending in awe-inspiring cascades down 2,000m of walls and slabs. The smashed and distorted trees at the foot of the mountains tell their own tale.

Unless otherwise mentioned, crampons are rarely necessary on any of the summer snow routes but an ice axe can be a wise precaution on some of the glaciers and higher snowfields such as the approach to the top of the Troll Wall from Stigfoss.

Most of the peaks have been ascended in winter but weather conditions are then unreliable and the snow is usually poor. In the 1965–66 winter three climbers were killed by an avalanche when attempting Fiva Route. Due to continuous intense cold, during the whole of the 1966–67 winter there were only two weeks when crampons could be used. Ice-fall climbing is however increasingly popular and many of the big wall climbs have also been done in winter. (Some ice-fall climbs are described, climbed in the winters between 1970 and '79.)

Rock

The whole of the area is of metamorphic origin. The lower halves of the mountains have been polished by the glaciers. The result is 2,000m faces of rock, usually involving 600–1,000m of slab work (often vegetated, with difficult route finding through overlaps and impossible bulges) steepening above to the upper and cleaner 600–1,000m summit walls. Much of the best rock is on these upper faces and consequently the shorter 300–600m routes starting from the high valleys are good introductions to the area. These shorter climbs are usually steep, with good holds and in fine situations.

There are also some excellent climbs on the lower glaciated slabs such as Hornaksla, opposite Trollryggen and (a little further from the road) Norafjell at the northern end of the Trolltind massif. Additionally, there are numerous easily accessible large boulders providing excellent problems. Those below Mjølva Crag and Hornaksla are nearest to town. Further up the Romsdal valley (where the weather is usually good) are two excellent riverside locations. Skiri is 23km up the road (3km past Marstein) and Slettafoss is 37km from Åndalsnes.

The colour of the rock gives a good general guide to its nature. White, or very light coloured rock, is invariably overhanging and loose. Black rock is usually extremely difficult to climb if not impossible. The best seems to be the grey. Whatever the colour, peg cracks are very often poor, being frequently shallow or choked with moss or quartz. Fortunately, it is some of the steepest walls that have the best cracks!

Mountain Rescue

There is a rescue team which has carried out summer and winter rescues from the Troll Wall and elsewhere, but this is not the Alps; the team may not be instantly available and circumstances can make rescue difficult and lengthy. You should go into the mountains expecting to rely on your own resources if you can. If not, in case of emergency, contact the police on 71 22 11 11 or use the emergency number:112.

Before going out into the mountains it is prudent to leave details of the intended route and probable time of return. It is also sensible to carry a first aid kit and know how to use it!

Maps, Guidebooks and Mountain Info

Norway

The Norwegian Tourist Board (NTB) is, as they say, friendly and well organised. They have offices throughout Norway. You can also contact them in London at:
Charles House, 5–11 Lower Regent Street, London SW1Y 4LRX.
Tel: 0906 302 2003 (brochures), tel: 020 7839 2650 (info),
website: www.visitnorway.com.

A very useful alternative source of mountain info is:

DNT: Den Norske Turistforening/Norwegian Mountain Tourist Association. This organisation knows all there is to know about mountain trekking in Norway. They mark the trails with the ubiquitous red capital T, build the essential bridges and run the excellent hut system, the most accessible providing meals as well as self catering as in the smaller huts. The smallest are unstaffed. Their huts and trails are marked on the excellent 1:50,000 M711 and 1:100,000 Turkart maps. Contact: DNT, PO Box 7 Sentrum, Storgt. 3 0101 Oslo. Tel: (+47) 2282 2822, email: turinfo@dntoa.no, website: www.dntoslo.no.

Or, in Bergen, it's worth visiting the DNT Office, Tverrgaten 4/6, five minutes walk from the famous fish market (which is only five minutes from the international ferry terminal). For information on the numerous camping and chalet (*hytter*) sites throughout Norway, check out www.camping.no.

The M711 Map Series published by Statens Kartverk covers the whole of Norway at 1:50,000. A complete map list and an excellent and very informative brochure on Norway is available on request from the NTB. Maps and guidebooks and a wealth of mountain information will also be found at DNT.

For walking in Norway, unless you can read Norwegian, the best book is the 1997 Cicerone Press guide to *Walking in Norway* by Connie Roos, ISBN 1 85284 230 X. Unfortunately, it does not cover Romsdal apart from walks in the Southern and Eastern Ranges around Snøhetta (just outside Romsdal) and Pytteggen, Romsdal's highest summit. For other info on treks and climbs in the Norwegian mountains, you could try *Scandinavian Mountains* by Peter Lennon, Guide Collomb (West Col, ISBN 9 06227 32 1) or the *Rother Walking Guide Norway South* (2000, ISBN 3 7633 4807 7). For more general information on walking in Norway, refer to *Mountain Hiking in Norway* by Erling Welle-Strand (1993, ISBN 82 90103 64 6).

For interesting historical background reading, check out *Norway, the Northern Playground* by W C Slingsby, just republished by Ripping Yarns (2003, ISBN 1 904466 07 9).

A couple of useful websites are: the Norwegian Alpine Club: http://www.ntk.no and http://www.steepstone.com/forere/andreforere.asp.

For general travel as well as a few selected treks, check out the informative *Rough Guide to Norway*.

Romsdal

For the Romsdal area in particular, there are two recommended maps at 1:80,000 with recent information on huts and trails. These are: Romsdalen Turkart, and Romsdalsalpene. Both are available from the Åndalsnes tourist office, or bookshops in Åndalsnes such as Romsdal Libris, down the street from the post office. They have walking trails marked and give you a feel for the whole area, but the best maps are the 1:50,000: 1320-1 Romsdal, 1320-11 Eresfjord, 1320-111 Åndalsnes, 1320-1V Valldal. The 1:100,000 Dovrefjell Turkart map covers Eikesdal and the eastern part of Romsdal, all the way to Dovrefjell and Dombås and shows the huts and trails in this area.

Guidebooks are also available from Romsdal Libris and at: http://home.no.net/bjartebo/main.html and www.skirisport.com.

A recommended topo guide to climbing in Romsdal's mountains is *Klatring i Romsdal* by Anne Grete Nebell and Bjarte Bø (1995, ISBN 82 995032 0 5). It is mostly in Norwegian, with some

Walking signs are infrequent but improving in the Romsdal area

Åndalsnes and the Western Ranges from Isfjord

English, but you should find it very useful in combination with this book. It is available from Hotel Aak and Romsdal Libris. Climbers will also find the Norwegian magazine *Klatrefører for Norge*,1997, useful for its topos of some Romsdal cliffs and other Norwegian climbing areas. You may be able to get a copy from the publishers at Prinsens Gt 3b, 0152, PO Box 325 Sentrum, 0103 Oslo.

Trekkers and those considering ski-touring in Romsdal should also see *Fra Topp til Topp i Romsdal* by Iver Gjelstenli (1997, ISBN 82 91883 00 9) in Norwegian with some English notes. Iver has also written *Opplev Romsdal på Sykkel* which has 45 cycling routes on- and off-road, all with maps, but Norwegian text (ISBN 82 91883 01 7). As mentioned above, the only English walking guide other than this to describe any walks in Romsdal (but only in the southern ranges) is the 1997 Cicerone Press guide to *Walking in Norway* by Connie Roos. There are also Norwegian guidebooks for trekking in that area, available from the DNT.

Gradings and Descriptions of Routes

All the climbs in this guide are given an overall grade and, wherever possible, a pitch by pitch grade. At the time when this guide was originally written, back in the 1960s, few of the climbs above Grade IV had been done often and the majority of the routes of Grade V and above had only had a few ascents.

Apart from some additional walks, unless specifically mentioned, there are only minor alterations and corrections in this fourth edition. The grades have not been altered. Some variables in the grading and times quoted are therefore to be expected. Climbs done by Norwegian teams after 1970 are likely to be slightly harder in their grading than other routes in this book.

In deciding the overall grade of a route, consideration is given not only to the maximum difficulty, but also to the length and seriousness of the climb. For instance, the South Wall of Bispen and the East Pillar of Søndre Trolltind are both graded IV sup. The former is technically more difficult as will be seen from the individual pitch gradings but it is shorter and without undue seriousness, escape being possible from all belays.

With the exception of the VI sup climbs, the routes described are almost all entirely free though many have pegs for protection and belays. A few of the hardest require pegs for aid and may have an occasional artificial pitch eg the Eastern Diedre of Nordre Trolltind. All the climbs with an overall grade of VI sup involved a considerable amount of artificial work when the first edition of this book was published in 1970.

Some, in particular the Rimmon and Swedish Routes on the Troll Wall were later climbed free with crux pitches of English Grade 5c and 6a respectively (modern Norwegian Grade 6+ and 7– see below). Sadly, both of these once popular routes suffered massively in the 1997 rock fall and have not yet been repeated. Local climbers say 'It's chaos up there!'.

Individual pitches of climbs are graded in degrees from 1° to 6°sup for free pitches, and from A1 to A4 for aid pitches. The grades compare approximately with those in the Dolomites in the 1960s. As grades have changed over the intervening 30 years, your first routes in Romsdal using this book will therefore be something of a voyage of historical discovery! The following table from the original guide should help:

Route Grades

Grade I	Very easy scrambles, possibly with pitches of 1° or 2°.
Grade II	Scrambles and easy climbs. Rope sometimes necessary. Probably pitches of 2° or 3°.
Grade III	Climbs suitable for inexperienced climbers. Mainly 3°, possibly some 4°.
Grade IV	Mainly 4°, with pitches of 5° and sometimes 6°inf.
Grade V	Mainly 5° with any amount of 6°.
Grade VI	Mainly 6°, possibly with pitches of 6°sup and any amount of artificial.
Grade VI sup	Sustained 6° and 6°sup with any amount of artificial.

With both types of grading, qualifications of inf (inferior) and sup (superior) have been used to indicate low or high in that grade. The following will give an idea of these grades by British standards:

Free Climbing Grades

Grade 1° and 2°	Up to Diff	2/3
Grade 3°	Diff to V Diff	3/3c
Grade 4	V Diff to Severe	3c/4b
Grade 5°	Severe to VS	4b/4c
Grade 6°	VS to Hard VS	4c/5a
Grade 6°sup	Hard VS upwards	5a/b etc

Aid Climbing Grades

A1	Easy pegging
A2	Awkward pegging. Steep, overhanging and/or loose.
A3	Difficult pegging. Steep, overhanging and possibly loose with poor pegs.
A4	Very difficult pegging. Almost certainly overhanging and probably with very poor pegs on bad rock.

The introduction to the routes gives, wherever possible, information on the whereabouts of the climb, the line taken, its continuity and any objective dangers, together with the actual length of climbing (rather than vertical height), time required and overall grade. Norwegian grades are mentioned a couple of times in this book where routes have been graded by them after 1970.

They are approximately half a grade up on French grades and a full grade on the English. There is nothing above Norwegian Grade 7 in this guide:

Norway	UK	France	UIAA	USA
4+	3c	4c	V	5.5
5	4a	5a	V+	5.6
5	4b	5b	VI-	5.7
5+	4c	5c	VI	5.8
6	5a	6a	VI+	5.9
6	5b	6a+	VII-	5.10a/b
6+	5c	6b	VII	5.10c/d
7-	6a	6b+/6c	VII+	5.11a
7	6a	6c+	VIII-	5.11b/c
7+	6a/6b	7a	VIII	5.11d

Times, unless otherwise stated, are from the foot of the climb to the summit, no allowances being made for approach or descent. Any directions for ascent are given facing the climb; in descent, they are always given facing out.

Now, let's head for the hills...

Vengetind after snowfall

Graded List of Walks, Climbs and Scrambles

Walks

Lake Eikesdal Ranges

	Route
To lower Mardalsfoss viewpoint	28
To upper Mardalsfoss viewpoint	29
To Eikesdal from above Mardalsfoss	30
Isfjord to Eikesdal	31

The Isfjord Ranges

Walks in the Isfjord Ranges	33
Romsdal to Dovrefjell	34
Moanebba North East Ridge	42

The Romsdalshorn Group

Nesaksla North West Ridge	75
Mjølva North West Ridge	79
Blånebba North West Ridge	89

The Trolltind Group

Alnesdalen–Marstein	137
Langfjelldal–Vermedal	138

The Kongen Group

Kløvstien	220
Isterdal to Innfjord	221

The Finnan Group

Innfjord–Trollstig Pass	257

The Western Ranges

Valldal to Berill	274
Berill to Måndal	279

The Southern Ranges

Bjorli to Tafjord	291
Round Pytteggen	292
Kongsvoll to Snøhetta	296

Scrambles – Grade I

Lake Eikesdal ranges

Goksøyra Ordinary Route	4
Skorta and Lille Skjorta, North Side	6
Vikesaksa North Ridge	9
Agottind North Ridge	10
Kleneggen Ridge	14
Hoemstind	15
Hauduken	17
Nyheitind, from south or north	22

via Knorten	23
Sjødala via Nyheitind	25
from north west	26

The Isfjord ranges

Skarven	32
Strandafjell	35

The Vengetind Group

Søre Vengetind South Ridge	62

The Romsdalshorn group

Holstind North Ridge	94
South Ridge	95
Hornaksla East Ridge	121
Olaskartind West Ridge	125
Kalskratind North West Ridge	126

The Trolltind Group

Breitind West Ridge	139
Trollryggen Ordinary Route	155
Brurjentene	175
Brur Skar	177
Nordre Trolltind North Ridge	194
Storgrovfjell South East Ridge	211

The Kongen Group

Bispen South Ridge Ordinary Route	222
North Ridge	229
Dronninga North Ridge	242
Prinsessa north and south sides	247
Karitind North Ridge	248
Setnesfjell East Face	252
North East Ridge	253

The Finnan Group

Søndre Finnan East Ridge	261
Middagsfjell North East Ridge	266

The Western Ranges

Ringshorn North West Ridge	270
East Ridge	271
Storfjell North West Face.	272
Hesten and Lille Hesten	273
Grønnfonntind	275
Trollvasstind	280
Masevasstind	282
Nonstind	283

Middagstind 284
Trollstolen 286

The Southern Ranges
Pytteggen East Ridge 289
Karitind from Pyttbua 293
Karitind from Reindalseter 294
Benkehø 295

Scrambles and Climbs of II inf – II sup

Lake Eikesdal Ranges
Fløtatind East Side 7
Agottind South East Ridge 11
Agottind by Midtre Agottind 12
Juratind South East Ridge 19
   West Ridge 20

The Isfjord Ranges
Nyheitind West Ridge 24
Morgodalstindane Ridge Traverse 27
Klaua and Kyrketaket Horseshoe 39

The Vengetind Group
Store Vengetind North Ridge 43
   North East Spur 44
   East Couloir 45
   Gallery Route 48
Lille Vengetind North Ridge 57
   South Ridge 58
   West Ridge 60
The Vengetind Ridge 63
Kvandalstind North Ridge 66
   South East Ridge 68
   South Face 69
Torshammer East Wall 72
The Kvandalstind–Vengetind Ridge 74

The Romsdalshorn Group
Blånebba South East Ridge 90
The Mjølva–Blånebba Ridge 99
Romsdalshorn Ordinary Route 101
Lille Romsdalshorn Ordinary Route 110
Hornaksla West Face 123
Vengetind–Kvandalstind–Romsdalshorn
Horseshoe 136

The Trolltind Group
The Søndre Trolltind–Breitind–
Stighorn Ridge 151
Klumpen South East Ridge 152
Stabben West Face 153

North Chimney 154
Trollryggen South East Ridge 156
   West Ridge 167
Trollspiret East Ridge 169
Trollgubben South East Face 170
Brudgommen South West Side 178
Ugla South Side 180
Spørsmålstegnet South Side 181
Store Trolltind Ordinary Route 182
Søstrene Pinnacles 191
Setergjeitind South West Pillar 210
Stighorn North West Couloir 213
   South West Couloir 217
The Stighorn–Breitind–
Trolltind Ridge 219

The Kongen Group
Bispen South Ridge 223
Kongen Ordinary Route 232
   West Ridge 234
Dronninga Ordinary Route 241
The Bispen, Kongen and
Dronninga Ridge 256

The Finnan Group
Finnan South East ridge 258

The Western Ranges
Taskedalstind 276
Seterfjell 278
Middagshorn 285

Climbs of III inf – III sup

The Isfjord Ranges
Juratind North East Ridge Ordinary Route 18

The Vengetind Group
Kvandalstind North East Face 67
   West Ridge 70
Torshammer West Wall 73

The Romsdalshorn Group
Nesaksla South West Face, Right-Hand
Buttress 78
Romsdalshorn North Face 100
   South West Ridge 108
Lille Romsdalshorn South West Wall 115

The Trolltind Group
Søndre Trolltind East Pillar, Original Route 145
Trollkjerringa South Face 171
   South East Side 172

Store Trolltind West Ridge	183
by Høg Skar	184
by Lav Skar	185
Bjørka North Side	192
Trollklørne North Ridge	193

The Kongen Group

Bispen East Couloir	224
East Ridge, Original Route	226
East Ridge, Direct Route	228
Kongen South Ridge	233
Setnesjfell North West Ridge	254

The Finnan Group

Søndre Finnan South East Face	262
Midtre Finnan South Ridge	264
Østre Finnan South Ridge	265

Climbs of IV inf – IV sup

The Isfjord Ranges

Klauva South Pillar	40

The Vengetind Group

Store Vengetind East Wall	46
South Wall	49
South Wall and East Ridge	50
South West Gully	51
West Ridge	53
West Wall	55
Lille Vengetind South West Wall	59

The Romsdalshorn Group

Nesaksla South West Face, Original Route	76
Romsdalshorn East Ridge	102
West Wall Original Route	105
by Nasen and Gielet	106
by Altanen and Gjelet	107
Lille Romsdalshorn East Ridge	111
East Face, RAF Route	112
Hornaksla South West Slabs	124
Kalskratind South West Buttress	129
Mongefossen	131

The Trolltind Group

Breitind East Couloir	141
Søndre Trolltind East Pillar	149
Trollkjerringa West Wall	173
Brura South East Side	176
Store Trolltind North East Ridge	186
East Face, Fiva Route	187
Nordre Trolltind Central Ridge	201
Stighorn West Couloir	215

The Kongen Group

Bispen South Wall, Phoenix Route	225
Gråbeindiederet	227
Kongen East Face, Original Route	239
Dronninga East Face	243

The Finnan Group

Middagstind North East Ridge	268

Climbs of V inf – V sup

The Vengetind Group

Store Vengetind East Face	47
South Wall Direct	52
Drømmediedre	54

The Romsdalshorn Group

Nesaksla South West Face, Leaning Gully	77
Blånebba South Wall	91
Holstind South West Pillar	96
West Couloir	97
Romsdalshorn West Wall, Direct Route	103
Cross Climb	104
Lille Romsdalshorn South East Wall	113
South Ridge	114
Hornaksla South West Spur	117
Kalskratind South West Couloir	128
Vengetind–Kvandalstind–Romsdalshorn Horseshoe	136

The Trolltind Group

Breitind East Pillar	142
Trollkjerringa South West Wall	174
Brudgommen East Pillar	179
Nordre Trolltind South East Ridge	195
Eastern Diedre	196
East Face	198
Left-Hand Ridge	199
Hazucha Route	202
Adelsfjell South East Cracks	204
Adelsfjell Eastern Slabs	205
Norafjell South East Spur	206
variations	207
via Grunero	208
Stighorn West Wall	214
South West Buttress	216

The Kongen Group

Kongen South Wall, German Route	235
South Wall Variant	236
South East Face	237
Dronninga East Ridge	244

Setnesfjell South East Face, Ordinary
Route 249

Western Ranges
Taskedalstind 277

Climbs of VI inf – VI sup
Lake Eikesdal Ranges
Goksøyra North West Rib 2
    West Wall 3

The Isfjord Ranges
Moanebba South West Face 41

The Romsdalshorn Group
Mongejura South Wall 132
    West Diedre 133
    South Pillar 134

The Trolltind Group
Søndre Trolltind Høibakk's Chimney 146
    North Face, Left-Hand Dihedrals 147
    North Wall 148
Trollryggen South East Wall 157
    East Pillar 158
Troll Wall Norwegian Route 159
    Arch Wall 160
    French Direct 161
    Escape Traverse 162
    French Direct-Polish Variant 163
    Rimmon (English) Route 164
    Swedish Route 165
Nordre Trolltind, Dieska Route 200
Adelsfjell East Couloir 203
Norafjell, Future Games 209

The Kongen Group
Kongen East Face Direct 238
Setnesfjell South East Face Direct 251

The Western Ranges
Blåstolen North Wall 287

Right Edge. IV inf 38

The Romsdalshorn Group
Mjølva cliff, North Edge VI inf 80
    Outer Limits V sup 81
    Tarzan VII inf 82
    Tiger Sweat V sup 83
    Central Route V 84
    Outer Edge V 85
    The Diedre IV 86
    South Wall V inf 87
    Central Diedre VI inf 88
Hornaksla Crag, Ingrid Espelid V sup 118
    Gravrammer VI 119
    Super Crack VI 120

The Trolltind Group
Stigfoss Veggen, West Gully V 212

Glacier Climbs
Glaciers providing snow and ice climbing in the summer.

The Romsdalshorn Group
Kvandalstind, East Mjølnir Glacier 64
    West Mjølnir Glacier 65
Kalskratind, Uncharted Glacier 127

Finnan Group
Finnan, North East Glacier 260

Winter Ice

Lilleteigsfossen 297
Sdolåa 298
Skogagrova 299
Trollstigsfossen 300
Tverelva 301
Nyttårsisen 302
Left Innholmsice 303
Nonstind West Flank 304

Training Cliffs and Climbs
Routes not having summits as their final goal; sometimes short, always easy of access and descent, and convenient for an easy day.

The Isfjord Ranges
Skorgedal Lower Cliff, Central Route. IV 36
    Upper Cliff, Left Edge. VI inf 37

Lake Eikesdal Ranges

Juratind dominates the eastern skyline

Lake Eikesdal is one of the most beautiful mountain lakes in Norway. Sixteen kilometres long and one and a half wide it has a small road along its eastern shore to the small, isolated village of Eikesdal at its southern end. From here there is another small road which goes over the mountains to the east into Sundal, another famous mountain region. Walkers wishing to go to Eikesdal can take a track north east, just up the E136 from from Verma, in Romsdal, and through high mountain valleys (see Route 30). This covers a distance of 16km passing by the shores of some remote lakes. There is likely to be much snow on this approach until the end of June. Since hydroelectric work in the 70s, much of this is now driveable, almost up to the lake that feeds Mardalsfoss, the highest waterfall in Europe, so walking to this point is no longer necessary! The area is covered by the 1:80,000 Romsdalen map and the 1:100,000 Dovrefjell Turkart which extends east to Dovrefjell.

The dramatic big walls of Goksøyra loom impressively above the lake's northern end, whilst at its southern end, Mardalsfoss plunges 655m in two great falls, the upper of which is free for 292m. It is a truly impressive sight. For ten months of the year however, it is diverted into Romsdal's hydroelectric system, but from 20th June to 20th August it runs free. This is the time when the winter's snows are melting from the high mountains and the waterfall is in full spate with foam flying 100m into the air, making the scene unsurpassable. There are paths from the south west shore of the lake to the foot of the fall (Route 28) and from the hydroelectric scheme's gravel road to its top (Route 29).

At the northern end a well-known salmon river, the Eira, flows into the Eresfjord which is a side arm of the main Romsdalsfjord. It is from this end that most people approach the lake as here are good roads and a bus/ferry services to Molde on the coast, and to Åndalsnes, each about 80km away. The journey from Åndalsnes is about 1½ hours on roads 64 and 660 to Eresfjord.

For those who prefer a little walking another method of approach from Åndalsnes is, after driving to Søredal Seter via Isfjord and Grøvdal (18km), to walk for 12–15km over either of two mountain passes to Hoemsbu Hut on the western shore of the lake, or to Øverås in the north via Svartvassbu hut (see Route 33 in the Isfjord Ranges).

Accommodation and campsites will be found at the villages at either end of the lake. For those climbing on the Juratind peaks, it may be preferable to stay in Grøvdal. Otherwise, the only accommodation further along the eastern and western shores of the lake is at the farm of Vike and at Hoemsbu Hut respectively.

With the exceptions of the Juratinder, Goksøyra and the Mardalsfoss walks, the mountains in this area are seldom visited, access being a problem. Most of them are scrambles, though often with worthwhile summit ridges. Also, particularly in the area of Juratind, there are some glaciers. There are a few big unclimbed walls in this region, some particularly gloomy and forbidding ones being hidden away in dark corries above the lake. It is also likely that the mountaineer will find some uncharted ridges and climbs of a more average standard amongst these isolated peaks. The lowest south west buttresses of Goksøyra give good steep training climbs and other small crags have been developed, Håhammeren in particular offering some short technical slab climbs. This crag is situated right of the road, 2km from Eresfjord towards Eidsvåg (see *Klatring i Romsdal*). The main climbing attraction is undoubtedly Gokøsyra, which now has over ten routes. Those towards its left side were originally reached by the lower central couloir but are best reached by:

1. THE TERRACE APPROACH

Though the best way in, it's still long, taking 3–4 hours and including some easy climbing. Park below the face, on a small hill and walk up to and around some farmland, left of a mast. From there, a trail marked by red dots leads through the woods and up scree. Eventually, trend right up wooded ledges. When the red dots stop, there are two pitches (3) up a cliff to reach the top of Husmannen (the projecting wooded knoll). From there go out left to reach two easy pitches up to the terrace.

The original route on the wall was by a famous British team, the late Dr Tom Patey and the man known to British climbers as 'The Master' – Joe Brown:

Goksøyra 1,318m (4,328ft)

2. NORTH WEST RIB
(J Brown, T Patey. 1967)

Takes the easiest line up the Main Wall, meandering from right to left with unusually difficult route finding. The route begins in the obvious Slab Couloir in the lower right, and breaks out left at the obvious bulge, up the flank of the Valley Buttress

(Husmannen). It then crosses the upper left edge of the Amphitheatre to gain the indefinite North West Rib which marks the division between the upper face – The Curtain – on the right, and the easier angled receding wall above the dividing gully on the left. An excellent route with some very good climbing in exposed situations on the Rib. 7 hours, though many parties may require a bivouac. Over 1,500m. Grade VI.

Original approach (see preferred Terrace Approach above). Climb the Slab Couloir to the bulge, negotiating two 100m slabby inclines (the first 4°, the second also 4°, but with 7m of 6° at the top of the incline). Below the bulge, the gully bed trends round left towards a 70m overhanging chimney in the left wall of the couloir. Climb the vertical rib on the left of the chimney by two pitches (5°, 5°sup) to a lodgement on the tree-covered flank of the Valley Buttress. Here, the best route is far from obvious. Trend right for 40m (5°sup) and continue by numerous rock pitches (4°) for 240m to gain the Amphitheatre.

Walk left across the Amphitheatre to reach the ledge system low down (instead of tackling the rock barrier at the top of the

Amphitheatre). 240m of steep scrambling edging leftwards on grassy ledges then lands one at the foot of the North West Rib where rock climbing difficulties recommence. The Rib is tackled in a direct line towards the top, avoiding leftward diverging grooves.

Climb 30m to the top of a block (4°) and up the right-hand side of the rib for 25m to the top of a flake (4°), before making an airy traverse left for 7m (4°) across the vertical wall to a crack and chimney system. Climb this for 55m or so (5°) to a ledge (with a water trickle accessible on the left). Trend back towards the central rib line to reach a good ledge in 60m below a huge slab seamed with cracks. Some delicate and very exposed slab work follows for 15m (6°) to cross an edge into a hidden groove. This continues up the slab for a further 25m (5°sup) to a peg belay where the groove turns right and steepens. After a further 12m (6°, 1 peg), pull out left to a ledge. Turn the next wall on the left and return to a large ledge above where the angle eases slightly and holds become abundant. Trend right to savour the exposure of the Main Wall overlooking the Amphitheatre and climb more or less directly to the top in four rope lengths (4°, 4°, 5°sup, 3°) finishing 60m left of the summit cairn.

3. WEST WALL

(V G Hansen, K Storen, I Walaas. 1968)

An excellent climb attacking the centre of this beautiful face by its only obvious natural weakness. From the Terrace, the route follows two long crack lines diagonally right to finish in the Central Diedre and exiting 90m right of the highest point. The rock is very sound and gives extremely fine climbing. Nuts, T-chocks and American pegs (knife blade to 3" bongs) were used and

none left in place. To return in case of bad weather could be difficult but not extremely so. The first ascent was made in 16 climbing hours though a competent team should do the route in 10 hours from Husmannen. 1,350m (600m of actual climbing). Grade VI inf. Diag below.

To reach the start of the climb proper, ascend Husmannen up its forested front (see Terrace Approach, Route 1). Halfway up is 90m of climbing (2°,3°). 2–3 hours. It is advisable to bivouac here (no water). From Husmannen continue as the Brown-Patey route left across a rubble gully to the base of a big diedre. Go left, round the corner, then continue by 60m of scrambling in gullies and over slabs before moving right above the diedre to a large grass ledge. Cross this to its right end and up 18m to some blocks where the route really begins.

Climb for two rope lengths slightly right to the next grass ledge (2°, 3°) then up right for 15m to the first long crack which is in reality a big diedre ending in a roof. Follow this for a

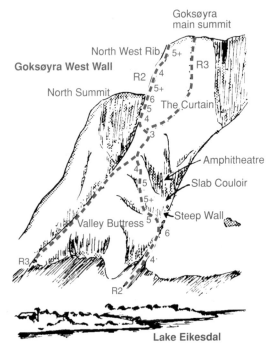

View east of Romsdalfjord to Kirketaket (left) and Juratind (right)

pitch (2°, 3°), then a rope length (4° A1, 3 pegs, 5°) then 25m (5°) to the roof. Pass this on its right (25m, 5°) to reach a small ledge, then directly up a vertical crack for 18m. (A2, 6 pegs, 5°). Above, a short rightwards pendulum and a few feet of climbing (6°) lead to a fine ledge. 9m higher are more good ledges with a possible bivouac site to the right.

Continue straight up for 30m by a diedre to the left of a big roof (5°) and belay to the left. Go up left again, then back right over a slab and up grooves for a pitch (4°, 5°inf) to the start of the second 'crack'. Following this for three pitches (3°, 4°) brings one to a big ledge at the bottom of the Central Diedre (possible bivouac). Ascend 18m to a ledge about 30m right of the diedre then slightly right again into a steep chimney. Up this for a pitch (4°sup) and move out right to a small ledge. Continue in the same chimney for another rope length (3°sup) then 18m right over blocks (4°) to the top.

4. ORDINARY ROUTE
(J Iverson and party. 1874)

A pleasant scramble. From Øverås follow the path along the shore of the lake and up the wooded hillside towards Ljøsebotnsaeter, leaving it for the south east ridge which leads without difficulty to the summit. Grade I.

5. DESCENT

Down the Ordinary Route. 1 hour

Skjorta and Lille Skjorta
1,715m (5,625ft)

This is the peak north east of Goksøyra. Its east face forms a steep precipice which terminates in a large cirque.

6. NORTH SIDE

The mountain can be ascended easily by the northern side, approaching from Eresfjord via Kvidal, or from Øverås via the Ljøsebotn track: either way 8km. Its neighbouring top, Lille Skjorta, is climbed by the East Ridge, from the East Col, from which the nameless east summit has also been ascended. Grade I.

Descriptive records of original ascents to the peaks on the eastern shore of the lake are all meagre. Little is known about them from a modern point of view, the following being the only information available in the old Norwegian Guide books.

Fløtatind 1,654m (5,425ft)

7. EAST SIDE
(V H Gatty, E Hande. 1899)

A long scramble with few obstacles. About 6–7 hours from Øverås. Grade II

Take the track to Lake Ljøsebotn and up into the snow-filled valley east of the northern outlier of Fløtatind. Continue southwards round snow slopes above the valley to the Storebre (Great Glacier). Now ascend by snow slopes to the long ridge of pinnacles which fringe the upper edge of the glacier and form the summit.

8. DESCENT BY THE SOUTH SIDE

Go down onto the southern side of the glacier and then northwards beneath the east spur of the mountain, back to Ljøsebotn and Øverås. 3–4 hours.

Vikesaka

9. NORTH RIDGE
(Hoem and Vike. 1910)

The ascent is merely a steep scramble. Grade I.

Agottinder 1,588m (5,209ft)

10. NORTH RIDGE
(An Eikesdal farmer. 1891)

The ascent from Vike to the north summit is merely an easy scramble. Grade I.

11. SOUTH EAST RIDGE
(B Goodfellow, E J Woolley. 1891)

An interesting climb. Grade II inf.

From Vike it is a long scramble into the Agotbotn cirque on the east side of Agottind with some loose rock. 'The edge above is so sharp that in some places the only method of progression is to sit astride the ridge with one leg dangling free.' A steep cliff about 3m high is surmounted by a narrow diagonal crack in the face of it, and the climb finishes at the south summit.

Midtre Agottind

12. RIDGE TRAVERSE
(H C Bowen, C W Patchell. 1896)

An interesting scramble. 6 hours. Grade II inf.

Follow Route 10 from Vike to the north summit beyond which the summit ridge is very sharp with a precipitous fall into Lake Eikesdal on the west. The passage of the arête to the south peak is completed in 2 hours and some of the rock is extremely loose.

13. DESCENT BY THE ORDINARY ROUTE

Cross the ridge from Søndre to Nordre and so down to Vike. About 4 hours.

Kleneggen 1,922m (6,304ft)

This peak, situated south of the lake, is the third highest peak in Romsdal and once had reindeer trails over its sharpest ridge.

14. THE RIDGE
(First ascent unknown)

Large sections of the ridge have tumbled down but the ascent is still easy. Grade I.

Information on the mountains on the west side of the lake is vague, most of the notes below being of first ascents.

Hoemstind 1,738m (5,701ft)

15. FROM HOEMSGJURA
(C Hall, Soggemoen and Norahagen. 1893)

Just a scramble. Grade I.

16.
(Aamot, Birkeland, Falkenthal and Hansen, 1939)

The eastern summit.

Haukelutind 1,650m (5,412ft)

This is said to be the twin-peaked ridge which connects with Hoemsgjura. Almost certainly it does not exist, being confused with another peak in pioneer accounts.

Hauduken 1730m (5,674ft)

17.
(H C Due and party. 1874)

An easy summit. Grade I.

Juratind 1562m (5,123ft)

18. NORTH EAST RIDGE, ORDINARY ROUTE
(I Kavli, B Moen and two shepherds. 1880)

A pleasant scramble with no real difficulties. 5 hours from the seter. Grade III.

The best approach to Søredal seter is from Åndalsnes, via Grøvdal. The route then goes easily up the broad ridge left of the glacier under its north wall and trends rightwards past small cliffs to its north top. The ridge is then followed to the main summit.

19. SOUTH EAST RIDGE
(F M Beaumont, A Bill, R B Caldicott, R S Rotherham, A Øverås, K and K Vike. 1899)

An interesting jagged ridge with several towers. 6 hours from seter, 5 hours from Hoem. Grade II.

The route starts from the highest part of the path between Søredal seter and Hoem, contouring across the glacier under the eastern side of the summit until the ridge is reached. This is then followed to the top.

20. WEST RIDGE
(H C Bowen and C W Patchell. 1903)

Pleasant scrambling on good rock, better than the North East Ridge, 6 hours from seter. Grade II sup.

Follow the path from the seter into the valley and then trend rightwards across the

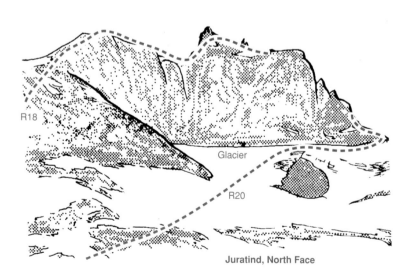

R18

Glacier

R20

Juratind, North Face

Espen Gjelstenli on Goksøyra West Wall

glacier to the gap in the West Ridge. Up this to the top, with some climbing, moving right to pass two steep cliffs about halfway.

21. DESCENT

By the Ordinary Route. About 3 hours.

Nyheitind 1,590m (5,215ft)

22. FROM SOUTH OR NORTH

This is the peak north of Juratind. It can be ascended easily by the south side from the Isfjord–Hoem path or by the north from the Isfjord–Øverås path.

23. NYHEITIND VIA KNORTEN

The route is without difficulty. Grade I.

24. NYHEITIND WEST RIDGE
(H Gruner, S Eide, H Doseth. 1976)

Not much climbing but a fine tour. Grade II

Sjødala 1,690m (5,577ft)

25. FROM NYHEITIND

Continue the ridgewalk eastwards, descending to a col before rising to the top of Sjødala.

26. NORTH WEST SIDE
(O Stavrand, A Gruner, B Østigard, K Svanemyr, H Doseth. 1976)

A pleasant scramble. Grade I.

Take the path up from Grøvdal to Svartvassbu and up to the scar on the north west ridge. Easy climbing follows from here then up snow slopes to the top.

These peaks are situated on the right side of Søredalen at the end of Grøvdalen in Isfjorden.

Morgodalstindane

27. RIDGE TRAVERSE
(B Østigard, S Eide. 1976)

The traverse of all the peaks. Grade II.

Before leaving this section it is essential to mention the walks to the magnificent Mardalsfoss:

28. WALK TO THE LOWER MARDALSFOSS VIEWPOINT

From Eikesdal at the head of the lake, take the signed road past campsites to a large car park 2km along the west shore of the lake and just beyond the bridge passing over the stream that descends from the falls. Follow the path up through the woods, passing another smaller car park area (trend right here) and eventually reaching the foot of the falls. Easy (though sometimes slippery on wet rocks). About 1.5km. About ½ hour and the same for the return.

29. WALK TO THE UPPER MARDALSFOSS VIEWPOINT

This walk is much more serious than Route 28. Its start is not obvious, nor is there a well-marked path and a bit of scrambling (and possibly snow) is involved. However, the view from the top is magnificent but don't be tempted to get too near – it's a glacially smoothed and rounded edge and a long way down! About 2km. Less than an hour from the road and the same for the return.

Approach by car, leaving the E136 between Åndalsnes and Dombås about 8km south of Verma at Kleiva (5km north of Bjorli). Just after passing under a railway bridge, take a gravel road left. This road (part of a hydroelectric project) turns left and rises up onto a high plateau via a series of switch-backs (it may be signed Mardalsfoss). After crossing a pass at 1,136m with some huts (good views) it follows the east shores of Sandgrøvvatn and some smaller lakes to its north, before bending left. It then follows the left side of a river with several hydroelectric installations, beyond which there is a small

lake on the left (Fossafjelltønna) and a lay-by on the right, after which the road continues round the lake before rising again northwards.

Leave the car at the lay-by (about 23km from the E136) and walk north on a path onto a rocky headland with streams below to left and right, and Mardalstjønna ahead. Scramble down the rocks and go left round the lake edge until forced up and left over a shoulder. Scramble down rock, scree (and snow) to reach the lake again and continue easily once more on a small path to its north end, where the river runs rapidly out, little knowing that in 50m it will plunge wildly over a 600m drop. Take care not to join it!

30. WALK DOWN INTO EIKESDAL FROM ABOVE MARDALSFOSS

Take the same approach by car as Route 28 as far as the left turn 1km after Sandgrøv-vatn and the smaller lakes to its north (about 21km, or only 1.5km back from the lay-by on the previous route). A path then descends, increasingly steeply, north east to Eikesdal at the south end of the lake. Good views on the descent. About 4km. 1–2 hours.

It is also possible to walk to Eikesdal from Bjorli via Finnset. Or, for a long approach on foot to the last two routes, check out:

31. WALKS FROM ISFJORD TO EIKESDAL

There are three trails from Isfjord over to Eikesdal starting at Grøvdal. The northern way goes via Svartvassbu to Øverås at the north end of the lake (15km). Another forks right (south east) off the Svartvassbu trail after 5km, over the hills to Hoemsbu on the west shore of the lake (about 12km). The other possible walk (which is long and has no huts en route) shares a common start but then heads south after 2km, first up through woods, then alongside a chain of lakes to a pass at 600m. There it meets the gravel hydroelectric road before descending slightly for 5km to the lay-by at Mardalstjønna (see Route 29). Distance about 23km. It then picks up the walk to Eikesdal (Route 30) for a further 6km making about 29km total.

The Isfjord Ranges

The Klauva pinnacles in winter garb

Isfjord is the inland extremity of the Romsdalfjord, with the village of Hen at its head. It is 6.5km east of Åndalsnes by road. Eleven kilometres further east is the Juratind Group, above Eikesdal, approached from Hen via the Grøvdal valley and described in the previous section.

The other major valley from Hen is Erstaddal to the south east, which has a road along it as far as the entrance to Kvandal. Due south of Hen is Vengedal. All these peaks south of Hen are dealt with in the Vengetind and Romsdalshorn sections. Apart from Moanebba, the mountains in this section are all north of Isfjord and are pleasant walking (and skiing) country, with some small cliffs and the excellent climbing area of Klauva. There are a number of tourist huts near fishing lakes, providing accommodation at Måsvassbu, Vasstindbu and Svartvassbu (the latter being on one of the Isfjord to Eikesdal walks, see Route 31 and Route 33). The area also provides excellent winter skiing.

Skarven 1,048m (3,458ft)

This peak can be seen as a massive hump as one looks across the fjord from Åndalsnes. It is mostly visited during March, April and May when there are excellent skiing conditions with a ski tow south east of the lake on Strandafjell. It is 8km by road from Hen to Skorgedal which is the approach valley. A pleasant walk up this beautifully wooded dale brings one in 3km to the huts and fishing lake. You can drive to this point, paying a small toll at the 'honesty box'.

32. SKARVEN EAST SIDE

The summit affords excellent views of Åndalsnes, the Romsdal mountains and fjord. 3km. Grade I.

33. WALKS IN THE ISFJORD RANGES

From the huts by Selseter Lake in Skorgedal there is a path north east up Ljøsadalen from which a return walk is possible through Breiviskaret to Isfjord (about 15km) or turn left near the head of Ljøsadalen (where the Breivikskar route goes south) and continue through high mountain valleys to the north east, to Måsvatn, a well known fishing lake with Måsvassbu tourist hut on its shore (about 15km). From Måsvassbu it is then possible to continue along trails first to Vasstindbu (11km), then Svartvassbu (8km) and link into the northern trail from Grøvdal to Eikesdal (8km) making a three-day walk. From Svartvassbu you can also walk back to the road in Grøvdal (7km) and thence to Isfjord. There is also a route from Måsvassbu directly to Isfjord over Loftskar (14km).

34. ROMSDAL TO DOVREFJELL

Peter Lennon, in his book *Scandinavian Mountains* (see section: Maps, Guides and Info on Norway) suggests a multi-day trek starting from Isfjord, as follows: Grøvdal – Hoemsbu – over Lake Eikesdal to Vike – Reinvassbu – Aursjøhytta– Grøvudalshytta – Amotdalsytta – over Snøhetta to Reinheim – Kongsvoll (probably seeing muskox on the latter section). This walk could be extended a couple of days by starting from Skorgedal via Måsvassbu and Svartvassbu. The route is covered by the 1:100,000 Dovrefjell Turkart.

Strandafjell 790m (2,607ft)

35.

Like Skarven, this peak is popular for skiing at Easter. It is along the northern shore of Isfjord, best approached from Skorgedal where there is a car park and ski tow (see approach for Skarven). It is easily climbed in summer and is a good view point. There is a higher top is to its east, Breidvik, 900m (2,970ft).

Skorgedal

The valley of Skorgedal is immediately opposite Åndalsnes, across the fjord. It is less than 2km away by boat, but 14.5km by road via Hen. Looking from Åndalsnes, two cliffs can be seen projecting from the wooded western hillside of the dale. Both are only a matter of minutes from the road which runs up the valley and are worth a visit if the weather is bad in the mountains (or just for an easy day). There are excellent views across the fjord and the journey is all the more worthwhile if one crosses the fjord by canoe!

Skorgedal – Lower Cliff
36. CENTRAL ROUTE
(A Howard, R Holt and J Murray. Winter 1967)
T Fosse and party have also done a route on this cliff following a similar line.

A vegetated start with better climbing above, beginning right of centre on grassy rock with a mass of unclimbed smooth slabs to its right. 150m. Grade IV

Ascend one rope length straight up to a good ledge (3°), then trend left into a steep groove which is climbed with a peg (5°sup). Delicate climbing left across slabs (5°) leads to the central corner; cross this (wet) and up a groove to trees. Broken rocks to the top (4°).

Descent The best descent is to abseil down the slabs using trees, left of this route.

Skorgedal – Upper Cliff
37. LEFT EDGE
(A Howard, R Holt. Winter 1967)

A wandering and somewhat false line but combining some interesting and fairly difficult pitches. 150m. Grade VI inf.

Climb directly up slabs to the huge white overhang (4°), then over it by a groove near its left edge (2 pegs), followed by delicate climbing up left across a wet loose groove and slabs (6°) to a ledge. Up the slab above, and over a roof (2 pegs) then delicately up and right (6°) to a ledge in a vegetated groove. Broken rocks above to the top (4°).

Descent The most entertaining descent is to abseil straight down this groove and over the overhang, using convenient trees.

38. RIGHT EDGE
(A Howard, R Holt. Winter 1967)

An enjoyable route up slabs with excellent holds. 120m. Grade IV inf.

Climb directly up slabs to the huge white overhang (4°) then traverse right, beneath the roof, on good holds and straight up (4°). Left a little, then slant right up slabs and over a bulge (5°) to more broken rocks near the top.

Descent Abseil left of the route.

Klauva and Kyrketaket
1,500m (4,920ft)

Easily seen from Åndalsnes, looking north east, this is the location of a nice climbing area with a nearby hut run by the local Romsdal Tindegruppe. The climbs are mostly of high quality made in the last 20 years or so. There is also a good ridge walk here over Kyrketaket ('the Church Roof').

39. HORSESHOE RIDGE
(J and C Lysholm. 1911)

A pleasant ridge walk. 10 hours. Grade II inf.

This ridge system is 5km north east of Hen and gives a very enjoyable day in the mountains. Follow the track to Måsvatn as far as Loftskar seter (4km), from which the horseshoe ridge may be taken in either direction, with some climbing on the Klauva Pinnacles which give 2° scrambles. Beneath the pinnacles a 300m broken wall drops into the valley.

The Klauva peaks are a very fine group, with good solid rock, discovered by local climbers in 1978. The approach is by the Måsvassbu track to Loftskar seter then south east, uphill towards Skarven (not the Skarven near Skorgedal!). After about 200m or so of ascent, contour east on a small path to the climbers' hut, Stall'n, about 3 hours. Then it's another hour or so to reach the climbs

Klauva and Kirketaket

Springtime skiing in the Isfjord mountains. Romsdalsfjord and the Western Ranges in the background

There are now many fine routes on the different pinnacles. The first of these was:

40. KLAUVA SOUTH PILLAR
(B Amundsen, F Martinsen, H Doseth. 1978)

This route goes up the right side of the yellow slabby pinnacle in the centre of the main South Pillar. 5–6 hours. 300m. Grade IV.

The first rope length, which is the hardest, goes up a diedre (5°inf) and then traverses right into an easy gully (4°). Up the gully for two rope lengths and then onto the ridge again which is followed by the most natural way for three rope lengths (4°inf). The route ends on the top of a pinnacle.

Descent Abseil down on the right side into a gully which is followed to the ridge.

Details of other climbs on Klauva will be found in *Klatring i Romsdal.*

Moanebba 745m (2,444ft)

41. SOUTH WEST FACE
(A Howard, R Holt. Winter 1967)

This peak is 5km south east of Isfjord. Being at a low level it is in condition very early in the year, but this is a poor route with much vegetation. NOT RECOMMENDED. The climb starts below the left side of a cluster of roofs in the left centre of the face. 5–6 hours 600m. Grade VI inf.

Climb as directly as possible to the roofs, beginning in a wet overhanging groove (6°sup). Pass the roofs by an overhanging crack on their right (6°) then trend left before going straight up (5°, 3°) to finish exactly at the summit cairn.

Descent 30 mins by:

42. THE NORTH EAST RIDGE.

This is the usual approach to the tops of this group which are pleasant and easy walking country with good views of Vengedal, Kvandal and their impressive mountains.

The Vengetind Group

Vengetind West Face in winter

This is a fine ridge of Alpine peaks, including the highest summit in the central massif and providing some first class mountaineering routes, at all standards on some of the best rock in Romsdal. Vengetind is considered by many to be the most beautiful mountain in Romsdal. Slingsby described Kvandalstind, somewhat enthusiastically, as 'the steepest mountain in Europe'.

The usual approach is from Vengedal, which is 18km from Åndalsnes by car, the last 8km being by a toll road with 'honesty box'. There is another approach, this being by Kvandal which is a parallel valley to the east, on the other side of the Vengetind ridge, but this dale is seldom visited by anyone. It is nevertheless, the easiest approach to Kvandalstind. A car can be driven to Dale in Erstaddal (16km from Åndalsnes) where a footbridge over the river is followed by an 8km walk up Kvandal to the Mjølnir Glacier beneath the mountain's north east face.

Camping is possible anywhere in the high mountain valleys. Another facility is a marvellous stone shelter complete with door, window and fireplace, constructed under a boulder on the north side of Hornvatn. This is the lake at the head of Vengedal. Higher in the mountains between the southern ridges of Romsdalshorn and Søre Vengetind is Olaskar Lake which is reported to have a shelter on its northern shore.

Store Vengetind 1,843m (6,045ft)

43. NORTH RIDGE
(Hall, Norahagen, Soggemoen. 1882)

A long route but with no real difficulties.
5 hours. Grade II. Diag pg 49.

From the lower end of the Vengedal Lake, cross the wooded hillside and ascend an easy angled snow gully to a col on the North Ridge. Follow the ridge, keeping left, then moving right at halfway, the last 100m giving some scrambling (2°).

44. NORTH EAST SPUR
(W C Slingsby, J Vigdal. 1881)

A poor route, mostly on snow and seldom repeated. Grade II.

45. EAST COULOIR
(C and J Lysholm. 1912)

Rarely used nowadays, the climb follows gullies and slabs on the right of the main east face and finishes by the North East Ridge, Grade II.

46. EAST WALL
(O Mork, O Nesje. 1959)

No description is available to this route, but it would seem to go up the obvious central couloir. About 300m. Grade about IV sup.

47. EAST FACE ROUTE
(S Cathcart and M Slaney. 1975).

The climb involves an approach from Dale, finishing up snow slopes which lead to the main gully below the face. From the end of the gully, take the slabby left wall, then out onto the slabby right wall of the East Face cwm, to bivouac. The rest of the route is high standard climbing. A full day. 300m. Grade V sup.

Approximately 75m above the bivouac is an obvious right to left diagonal crack splitting the face. Climb the steep slabs and wall above to the centre of the crack (6°). Follow the crack left to near its end (6°). Gain the bottomless corner above via a thin crack passing a large loose block. Climb the corner with the aid of pegs (25m, 6° and A2). Move right with tension onto the steep wall and climb a shattered crack and groove above to a large block belay. Move left and up flakes (6°inf) ending on the 'Gallery Route'. Move left along the gangway to a narrow couloir. Follow the couloir relatively easily (5°) to gain the West Ridge near the summit. A bivouac was made near the foot of the North Ridge on the descent.

48. GALLERY ROUTE
(E Birkeland and party. 1925)

An easy, enjoyable mountaineering route with fine situations and mountain scenery. 5 hours. Grade II.

From Vengedal Lake scramble up the hillside to the great west snow gully which leads to the scar between Store and Lille Vengetind. The snow can be in dangerous avalanche condition in the very early season. Late in the season it has been known to give 600m of crampon work! The scar can also be

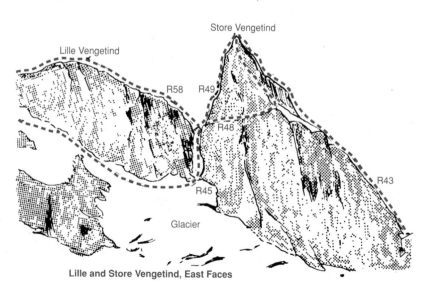

Lille and Store Vengetind, East Faces

reached over Søre and Lille Vengetind, or by a snow gully in the east face.

From the scar an easy, long 'Gallery' leads across the middle of the east face, high above the glacier to the north east ridge which is followed to the top.

49. SOUTH WALL
(A R Heen, O Hatlen, B Tokle. 1943)

A good rock climb in a fine situation, starting 20m down the west gully from the scar between the twin peaks. 6 hours from the seter, 2 hours from the scar. 180m. Grade IV sup. Diag pg 49.

Up a slabby gully to a large ledge, then leftwards past a large detached brown block. A difficult wall is then climbed followed by two more large ledges before moving left over a rough slab and up a steep gully to a further ledge. Descend a little and traverse the wall on an inclining ledge to a platform on the west ridge where a difficult 7m wall

leads to a shelf. Continue by a narrow gully and a difficult traverse to a hollow, from which a difficult overhanging wall brings one to the west ridge, just below the summit.

50. SOUTH WALL AND EAST RIDGE
(A R Heen, K Grønlund. 1935)

A more natural, easier line than the South Wall. 1½ hours from the scar. 180m. Grade IV inf.

Follow the South Wall to the ledge above the steep gully and then move out rightwards across large ledges to finish right of the summit.

51. SOUTH WEST GULLY
(R Høibakk, T Engvig. 1960)

No description is available. As far as is known the climb begins in the west gully and traverses in near the summit to join the south wall climb. Grade about IV sup.

Springtime view south up Vengedal to Vengetind

52. SOUTH WALL DIRECT
(Climbers from Molde)

A route is reported straight up this face with a sling for aid near the summit. Grade V sup.

53. WEST RIDGE
(E Heen, K Oshaug. 1930)

A classic mountaineering route and by far the best climb of its grade on the mountain. 7 hours from the seter. 600m. Grade IV inf.

Scramble up the hillside from the lake towards the mouth of the west gully which is on the right of the West Ridge. Gain the ridge without real difficulty and follow it easily until it steepens, level with a 2m detached block. Trend left for a rope length across a steep cracked slab and then traverse rightwards over a short difficult slab. Two rope lengths follow up the prominent and easy gully before moving left over the ridge to a spacious shelf. Continue up a difficult steep slab (peg) to a small hollow (often wet), then left across two steep crags and past a small pinnacle to the 'seven metre wall'.

This can be bypassed easily to the left by moving across to the North Ridge. Taken direct it is the route's most difficult pitch. Swing over the edge to the right and ascend via a ledge to the summit.

54. DROMMEDIEDRET
(H C Doseth, B Østigård. 1984)

This excellent and now classic route climbs the obvious corners to the left of the West Ridge. See Klatring i Romsdal. *Norwegian Grade 5-.*

55. WEST WALL
(First ascent unknown)

The route starts 40m left of the West Ridge and follows an impressive corner up to a big ledge often with snow. From the right of the ledge it goes rightwards on beautiful cracked slabs. (Almost as good as the West Ridge.) 300m. Grade IV sup.

56. DESCENT BY THE NORTH RIDGE

After initial scrambling it is often possible to glissade almost the whole of the way down into Vengedal. 2 hours.

Lille Vengetind 1,820m (5,970ft)

57. NORTH RIDGE
(W C Slingsby, W Ecroyd, E Norahagen. 1884)

A long mountaineering route with few difficulties. 5 hours from the seter. Grade II. Diag pg 49.

Ascend the west gully to the scar between the two peaks (Route 48) and then follow the north ridge to the summit.

58. SOUTH RIDGE
(A R Heen, K Grønlund. 1935)

The start is from the col between the Lille and Søre tops. Access to this is usually from Søre though it can be gained directly from the snow gully on the west. ³/₄ hour from the col. Grade II. Diag pg 49.

The route follows the sharp ridge directly to the summit. There are numerous pinnacles.

59. SOUTH WEST WALL
(A R Heen, B Tokle, O Hatlen. 1943)

Enjoyable on good rock, approached via the South Ridge from Søre Vengetind. 2¹/₂ hours. Grade IV.

From the ridge, descend left beneath the large, light coloured patch, above which the wall rises steeply. Start by ascending a long ledge towards the South Ridge, then left by a steep wall and ledge to a steep gully which is climbed on good holds in a very airy position. A further rope length trending left leads to the final gully and the summit.

60. WEST RIDGE
(First ascent unknown)

Mostly scrambling. 5 hours from seter. Grade II.

After ascending the hillside from Vengedal Lake the climb follows a complex system of broken ridges up the west face.

61. DESCENT BY THE NORTH RIDGE

Some scrambling down to the scar (¾ hour) from which it is usually possible to glissade most of the way down the West Gully, taking care at the exit onto the hillside. 2 hours.

Søre Vengetind 1,799m, 5,901ft

62. SOUTH RIDGE
(C Hall, M Soggemoen. 1898)

Very seldom climbed except as an approach to Lille Vengetind. 5 hours from Vengedal seter. Grade I.

Walk up Vengedal to Hornvatn, and up the scree slopes on its west flank to the foot of the east face of Romsdalshorn. Exit eastwards from the corrie (often snow) to Olaskar Lake on the plateau above the south rim of Vengedal. Continue round the lake to the south ridge which is followed easily to the summit.

63. THE VENGETIND RIDGE
(First traverse unknown)

An excellent mountain excursion crossing all three peaks and numerous intermediate pinnacles. From the seter and back, 11–13 hours. Grade II.

Follow the south ridge route to Søre Vengetind (I) and on along the summit ridge to Lille Vengetind (II) and down to the scar from which take 'The Gallery' to Store.

To increase the difficulty, many small climbs can be included on the pinnacles and of course the two south walls can be climbed.

64. EAST MJØLNER GLACIER
(B Østigard, A Gruner, K Svanemyr, H Doseth, S Eide. 1976).

Not much climbing, but a fine and recommendable route. The most difficult part is the start of the icefall which offers some ice climbing of about 60°. Norwegian Grade 4.

Start up Kvandalen and take the middle of the three glacier arms. The climb ends on the scar between Store Vengetind and Kvandalstind.

65. WEST MJØLNER GLACIER
(A Gruner, K Svanemyr, B Østigard, H Doseth. 1977).

A very nice route. Some ice-climbing of 60°. A long day. Norwegian Grade 4.

The route starts up Kvandalen and takes the right of the three glaciers, finishing at the scar between Store and Lille Vengetind.

Descent Return down the West Gully.

Kvandalstind 1,775m (5,822ft)

66. NORTH RIDGE
(W C Slingsby, C Hopkinson, I Jensen. 1885)

An easy and enjoyable mountaineering route in beautiful surroundings. 5 hours from Dale. About 450m. Grade II sup.

Walk up Kvandal and ascend the east snowfield, crossing over onto the North Ridge to join it at a shoulder just below the point where it steepens (possibly some difficulty at the bergschrund). Follow the ridge on good rock to the summit.

67. NORTH EAST FACE
(A Howard, K Chadwick. 1968)

A pleasant meandering route of no real difficulty but nevertheless enjoyable and in fine alpine surroundings. The route involves both rock and snow and the easiest way is not always obvious. 5–6 hours from Dale. 600m. Grade III.

Walk up Kvandal and continue as for Route 66 to the shoulder on the North Ridge. Move almost immediately right to a rake crossing the North East Face past snow slopes and under a white wall to chimneys (2°sup) leading to a col. Here is the pinnacle of

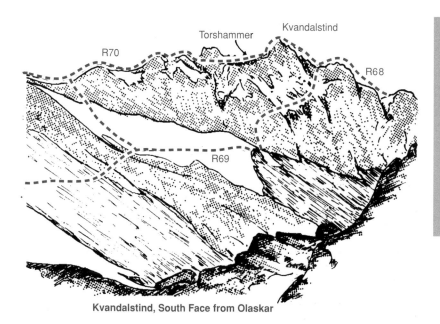

Kvandalstind, South Face from Olaskar

Hrungnir whose top can be reached easily but is dramatically situated above Mjølnir Glacier.

From the col continue along the rake until it ends abruptly. There now follows about 150m of pleasant climbing (2°sup) straight up a broken buttress on rock and snow until overlapping walls are seen just above. Escape left at the best point (not obvious) and ascend a groove to exit on the right edge of a snowfield (3°inf). Slant slightly rightwards for about 60m (2°sup), first up a cracked slab, then a grooved slab to steeper walls.

Ahead is a steep and fairly obvious chimney; do NOT climb this but instead traverse about 9m right and ascend by steep blocks trending right, then left, onto slabs for a rope length (3°). Another rope length trending slightly right (3°) leads to a recess. Pass this on its left then traverse back right above it and up to ledges (3°). Continue by a pitch traversing right (exposed) and ascending slightly (3°) to a ledge on the skyline. Above is the final steep and impressive wall which gives a superb finishing pitch (3°sup), first up a groove then a short traverse right into a bottomless chimney which exits on the West Ridge just 9m from the summit.

68. SOUTH EAST RIDGE
(H C Bowen, C W Patchell. 1896)

A good pinnacled ridge climb in a fine situation described by its pioneers as 'the finest rock climb in Europe'. 5 hours from Dale About 360m. Grade II sup.

From Kvandal, go leftwards across the sloping glacier to the lowest point on the south east ridge. About halfway up the ridge a large wall can be taken directly or passed to the left (3°inf).

69. SOUTH FACE
(W N Tribe, E Norahagen. 1893)

A long approach from Vengedal, and then mixed climbing. 6 hours from seter. About 360m. Grade II sup.

Walk from Vengedal, up to Olaskarvatn (Route 62) and contour beneath Søre Vengetind to a point above the north east shore of Svartvatn (the Black Lake). From here, move up across the snowfield to gain the buttress in the middle of the south face. Ascend this, moving right into the main gully and continuing rightwards to the obvious gap in the South East Ridge. Up this for three rope lengths to the top. Before reaching the gap, it is also possible to climb straight up by a shallow gully reaching the ridge about one rope length from the top. This is a slightly harder variation.

70. WEST RIDGE
(C and J Lysholm. 1920)

Kvandalstind's longest and most popular ridge, with a good steep finish. 6 hours from seter. Grade III inf. Diag pg 54.

The usual approach is as for Route 69 to the snowfield above Svartvatn whilst the lake can also be reached directly from Horgheim in Romsdal by the long, steep, vegetated gully which leads to Olaskar. The latter way is NOT RECOMMENDED.

From the snowfield it is an easy scramble up to the lowest col on the ridge between Kvandalstind and Søre Vengetind. Alternatively, the col may be gained from Kvandal by crossing the Mjølnir Glacier if conditions are favourable (the ice-fall can present difficulties).

From the col follow the ridge keeping to its south side and passing beneath Torshammer pinnacle. Beyond here the ridge steepens and gives good climbing to the top, moving right at difficulties.

71. DESCENT.

Almost any of the above routes, though the North East Face is complex. (If the South East Ridge is descended, one short abseil may be necessary from the lowest pinnacle.) 3–5 hours to Vengedal seter or Dale.

Whichever route you take up Kvandalstind, the inclusion of Torshammer is a 'must'.

Torshammer Pinnacle

72. EAST WALL
(E Fjeld, S Suhrke. 1925)

The easiest way up the unusual pinnacle on the west ridge of Kvandalstind. 27m. Grade II sup.

From the foot of its east side climb up by small ledges until it is possible to exit through a narrow hole onto the western side, and so to the top.

73. WEST WALL
(E Birkeland, P Langdal. 1930)

A steep and interesting climb. 27m. Grade III inf.

Climb directly up the steep west side on good holds.

Descent by abseil.

74. THE KVANDALSTIND–VENGETIND RIDGE
(First traverse unknown)

A long and interesting ridge system and a very worthwhile expedition. From and to Vengedal seter, 14–16 hours. Grade III sup.

The summit of Kvandalstind may be reached from Vengedal via the West Ridge or South Wall. To include the complete ridge it is best approached from Kvandal via the South East Ridge (II sup). Descend by the West Ridge (III inf) and on up to the summit of Søre Vengetind before descending to the col below Lille Vengetind. One can now avoid the next section of the ridge by crossing the glacier under its east face before ascending the snow gully to the scar under Store. Time permitting, it is more entertaining to go over the summit of Lille (II). From the scar, ascend 'The Gallery' on the east face and up to the top of Store Vengetind (II).

Fast moving parties may prefer to add interest (and difficulty) by including Torshammer and the Vengetinder south walls en route.

Descent is by the North Ridge.

THE VENGETIND–KVANDALSTIND– ROMSDALSHORN HORSESHOE.

See Route 136 for details of this superb three-day expedition.

The Romsdalshorn Group

Romsdalhorn from Vengedal in winter

This is an extremely long ridge of peaks rising out of Åndalsnes and forming the eastern perimeter of the Romsdal valley for 24km. The most dominant and unmistakable summit is the Romsdalshorn, one of the best known and most popular mountains in Norway. To its north are the lesser peaks of Holstind, Blånebba, Mjelva and Nesaksla, commonly known as Aksla which rises out of Åndalsnes. The highest summit, Kalskratind is south of the twin tops of the Romsdalshorn. South again is Mongejura. Most of the climbs in this group make a good introduction to the area in general, though the longer west face routes are more serious undertakings. There are some unclimbed big walls further up the Romsdal valley, as well as waterfalls giving possible winter ice-climbs.

The valley also has excellent bouldering, the nearest to town being Mjelva and Hornaksla below their eponymous crags. The other sites are further up the valley, where the weather is usually good, at the beautiful riverside locations of Skiri and Slettafoss, 23km and 37km respectively from Åndalsnes (see *Klatring i Romsdal*).

The usual approach to the climbs on the Romsdalshorn is, like Vengetind, from Vengedal and Hornvatn, 18km from Åndalsnes by road, the section up Vengedal being a toll road with 'honesty box' at the entrance to the valley. Most of the other peaks are usually climbed by their western faces, out of Romsdal, the start of the climbs often being less than an hour from the road. Some of the area's best 'cragging' and bouldering is here, on and below massive roadside cliffs like Mjølva and Hornaksla.

There are numerous campsites in Romsdal including one near Hornaksla (almost opposite the Troll Wall) and others nearer town. Hotel Aak is also in the main valley, on the E136, which is the main road from Oslo and close to the Isterdal junction. Descents from this group of peaks are usually via Vengedal, where there are bivouac huts and shelters that have already been mentioned in the Vengetind section. There is also a little hut on the top of Romsdalshorn.

For the walker it is a nice stroll up from Vengedal and on to Lillefjell, the saddle between Romsdalshorn and Holstind. There are superb views from here of the Vengetinder, Åndalsnes and the Trolltinder. The Trolltind Wall rises immediately opposite across the valley. Vengedal is also popular for skiers at Easter.

Nesaksla 842m (2,662ft)

(Locally known as Aksla)

75. WALK UP THE NORTH WEST RIDGE

Aksla's summit is a popular view point. An easy hour's walk from the town. It has been run up in 28 minutes!

The path begins at some wooden steps near the Europa Vei crossroads at the entrance to town from Romsdal, then follows the ridge.

Nesaksla Cliff

This is the south west facing crag visible from the south end of Åndalsnes, just below the top of Nesaksla. Due to its comparatively low altitude, it becomes climbable quite early in the season. The easiest approach is to leave the road out of Åndalsnes at the first railway bridge, and then straight up the wooded hillside to the bottom of the face.

76. ORIGINAL ROUTE
(A Howard, R Holt. Winter 1967)

A variety of pitches wandering up the corner left of the main slab, with impressive climbing up its continuation in the upper wall before escaping left through overhangs. A pleasant training climb. 5 hours. 450m. Grade IV.

Scramble leftwards up a pedestal into the corner then cross over and up ledges on its left to a large pine, regaining the corner by slabs (4°). Over an overhang (5°) then a long arc left and right into the corner again. Slightly left again, then a long traverse right under the roofs (5°) before going up grooves to 'the terrace'. A short corner crack (4°) leads into a recess with a huge steep slab on its left.

Follow a thin crack line 3m from the inner edge of the slab, gaining it with difficulty (5°sup). Escape left at the top through a groove onto slabs which go between roofs (4°) for 60m to the upper left edge of the wall, 120m of scrambling (2°) leads to the end of the rock, about 150m from the summit.

77. LEANING GULLY
(R Holt, D Ashton, K Stannard, D Little. 1967)

The route follows the obvious gully bounding the right edge of the main face. Enjoyable and high standard climbing on good rock. A good training climb, but not possible after wet weather. 4 hours. 270m, Grade V.

Scramble up to the base of the gully and climb it for 45m (5°) until the crack closes and it is possible to move left to a very thin crack. Start this with difficulty (5°sup) and continue directly up slabs for 75m until a good tree belay is reached to the left. Traverse right from the belay to a sloping ramp and climb this to the overhangs. Move left over the overhang and slab (3 pegs, 6°) and up into the groove to belay (6°). Ascend about 3m then move right (5°) to gain the main groove which is followed for 90m (4°) to the top.

78. RIGHT-HAND BUTTRESS
(A Howard, B Tweedale. 1967)

Not much good climbing but a pleasant and fairly easy route up the buttress right of the Leaning Gully. 3–4 hours. 300m. Grade III sup.

Scramble up to the base of the Leaning Gully and follow its left arête for 90m (4°sup, 3°), moving right on a good ledge beneath overhangs, and past a good tree belay. Take the next chimney on the right for another rope length (4°sup), then go right again and up a parallel fault for another pitch (4°). Right again and up a larger, more vegetated ramp for 90m (3°) to the top of the face. The summit is only five minutes away.

Descent is by the North West Ridge (Route 75). An easy walk ending almost in the centre of town! ½ hour.

In a hollow amongst pine trees on the western side of Aksla and only a few hundred metres above the road about 700m after the roundabout, is a 60m wall called H-Hammeren with a few grade 6 and 7 climbs described in *Klatring i Romsdal*.

Mjølva 1,215m, (4,010ft)

This is the next top south of Nesaksla.

79. NORTH WEST RIDGE

An easy walk along the tops from Aksla (Route 75) for a further 3km. The ridge then continues south east to Blånebba. The twin tops of Mjølva are about 2 hours from Åndalsnes. Grade I.

Down below, close to the road and Mjelva Camping, is:

Mjølva Cliff

From the gap between the twin tops, a long and impressive gully forms a straight gash down the western hillside. The lower part is bounded on both sides by Mjølva Cliff, a popular crag just over 3km from Åndalsnes and five minutes from the road. At the foot of the main cliff, which is left of the gully, is 'The Boulder' a 10m high block with over 20 problems, some very hard. Topos to these will be found in *Klatring i Romsdal*, together with topos to the many new and hard developments on this crag up to 1995.

80. NORTH EDGE
(B Tweedale, A Howard, 1968. Variation Start B Tweedale, J Greenwood, A Howard. 1968)

A vegetated and artificial line in that it seeks

The author on first ascent of South Wall, Mjølva, 1967

for rather than avoids the difficulties. Nevertheless, some hard climbing and fine positions. 4 hours. 300m. Grade VI inf.

Scramble up to below the left side wall of the main cliff on which an impressive hanging chimney will be seen. Climb slabs to the foot of the wall and up flake cracks (5°inf) to the roof. Traverse left to the lip with difficulty and ascend the chimney in a fine position to its top (18m 6°).

This point may be reached alternatively via the Variation Start: from the stone wall at the foot of the crag, scramble up slabs to an impending crack. Climb this for 18m (6°inf) to a hollow, then traverse left along a wooded rake and up cracks to the top of the previously mentioned chimney (18m, 4°sup).

90m of scrambling follows in an almost direct line past a bulging buttress at two-thirds height (3°) to a terrace beneath a massive leaning wall. From here take the

Halvor Hagen on Hull i Himmelen, 8+, Mjølva

groove in the right corner (15m 4°) onto the slabs and up to a grass hollow. Continue by a crack for about 6m (this can be followed to the top in three (3°) pitches), then make a leftward traverse descending slightly for 15m (5°sup) to a ledge on the upper lip of the leaning wall (peg belays). Continue along the lip to the left edge (exposed), then up slabs to a terrace (45m, 4°sup). Still following the left edge as nearly as possible, continue for two more rope lengths (3°) to the top of the crag.

Descent The easiest descent is to scramble left (north) through trees and across the stream above the waterfall. Two or three abseils down slabs, using trees, lead to the bottom of the gully.

81. OUTER LIMITS
(H C Doseth, R Amundsen, K Svanemyr. 1977)

About 5–10m right of the Hanging Chimney (Route 80). Follow the impressive crack on

the steep wall. A very good climb. Trees for abseil high up. 25m (5°sup).

82. TARZAN
(H Doseth, B Østigard. 1977)

Starts 15m left of the start of the Impending Crack on Route 80 alternative start. It follows the overhanging finger crack and is very difficult, but with good protection and good rock. 35m. Norwegian Grade 7-.

This unconventional grade was given in 1979 in the hope that other new ultra-hard climbs in Norway would not be confined into the old six grade system.

83. TIGER SWEAT
H C Doseth, B Østigard. 1977)

Starts up the Hanging Chimney of Route 80 then one rope length (25m) up a layback wall (5°sup) and a traverse right on a black slab (5°) to a ledge with small trees. Then up left to a small ledge and a long crack (5°inf) onto the black striped slab above. A difficult move follows to reach the crack above (6°inf) and follow it, then a hard move to traverse right to the next crack (6°). Follow it to the big tree ledge (4°).

Descent Abseil down from the left side of the ledge.

84. CENTRAL ROUTE
(R Fleming, J Finnigan. 1967)

The climb, which has some good pitches, follows the light coloured rib in the left centre of the face, finishing up slabs above. The start is about 30m left of The Boulder at the foot of an overhanging black slab. 3–4 hours. 390m. Grade V.

From a belay on the left of the slab move diagonally rightwards to a groove, which leads to slabs and a flake belay in a small corner (6°inf). 15m leftwards (3°) is a tree belay from which a steep loose crack goes back right to a ram, which is climbed for 27m (5°inf) to light coloured slabs on its left. An indefinite groove is then taken for 30m (3°) to a belay below and right of the steep light coloured rib before continuing up the groove for a further pitch (4°). Step delicately down left onto the crest of the rib and up the short steep wall (6°) and slab above (3°) for another rope length till below a steep black wall. This is climbed via a shallow groove on the right (5°) and then two rope lengths as directly as possible up slabs (5°) keeping just left of the vague groove. A pitch of scrambling follows to a belay by a prominent large straight tree beneath a belt of black overlapping walls. Move slightly right then trend left over a series of black overlaps (4°sup) to beneath a steep, undercut yellow wall. Tackle this in the middle, then traverse right above the overlap (5°) until it is possible to go straight up into a belt of trees.

Descent A descent can be made almost down the centre of the face using trees as abseil points.

85. OUTER EDGE
(A Howard, R Holt. Winter 1967)

An enjoyable climb with a variety of interesting pitches and some fine situations. Follows the right edge of the main slab mass just above and parallel to a long corner running the full height of the cliff – The Diedre. Both routes share the same start at a black slab. 3–4 hours. 480m. Grade V.

Delicately up the black slab (5°sup) for a rope length or, if wet, avoid it by a grassy groove to the right, reaching the same tree covered ledge. Move left and enter a concealed chimney which goes for 60m (4°) onto the outer edge of the main face. As the chimney fades trend right over slabs to gain a crack line which slants right near the outer edge for 90m (5°). A short overhanging section (6°) is passed at one third way, and an overhanging chimney at two thirds. Above, move left into a wooded bay, then back right to the edge which is followed for 90m (3°) to below an overhanging nose. Pass this by a steep crack on its right wall (6°) and continue up the crack line regaining the ridge just below another impasse. Avoid this on the right again by a steep wall (5°) then up the ridge above and finish by slanting right across a good grey slab (4°) to the top.

Descent To descend, scramble down the hillside to the right and into the Mjølva Gully or, before reaching the gully, abseil down the pillar on its left, from the trees. Good views from here of this climb, and of The Diedre, and the South Wall climb.

86. THE DIEDRE
(A Howard, R Holt. Winter 1967)

This is the obvious route running the full height of the cliff right of the main slab mass. It was the first route to be done on the cliff. Pleasant climbing though broken and vegetated in places. 3–4 hours. 420m. Grade IV.

Start up the black slab at the bottom right of The Diedre – delicate (5°sup), or if wet enter by the grassy groove on the right, moving left to the tree-filled nook. Follow The Diedre for 60m (4°) keeping close to its left wall, then make an interesting detour right through overlaps (5°sup) and up to below a large inverted V. Go up the V chimney and steep slabs (5°) to gain the upper diedre which is followed for 150m (3°) till it curves right for a rope length beneath overhangs (5°). Exit over the roof from the top of a pine tree! A further 90m (3°) leads to the top of the face.

Descent As for the Outer Edge (Route 85).

87. SOUTH WALL
(A Howard, R Holt. Winter 1967)

A tedious approach on slabs then excellent climbing up the steep light coloured wall right of and beneath The Diedre. Good positions and good rock. 3–4 hours. 360m. Grade V inf.

Ascend slabs beneath the wall, keeping left of a watercourse for 90m (4°sup) till at the foot of the wall. Up a grassy gully for 60m moving right to belay on slabs level with the upper side of the flake. Climb the flake crack (5°sup) to its top then traverse left in a fine position and enter a groove by a bulge (5°sup). Up the groove over another bulge (5°sup), then delicately rightwards across slabs (5°) into a concealed diedre. Up this till

Romsdal from Lillefjell

this crack to its end then step onto the wet black right wall of the corner and ascend this awkwardly to a belay ledge on the right wall (45m, 6°inf).

Ascend the right wall to a point where the corner is blocked, then traverse delicately right to a hidden groove which leads back into the corner. Continue up the steep corner with difficulty to a stance (45m, 6°). Still in the diedre follow it to an overhanging exit (2 pegs for aid) and belay 9m above (45m, 6°). The angle now eases and becomes more vegetated and two pitches (3°, 2°) lead to the top.

Descent Scramble across the top until at the Mjølva Gully. Follow the true left side of this down; no abseils.

near its top (4°) and escape by the left wall onto slabs and take the best line to the top (4°).

Descent as for Route 85.

88. CENTRAL DIEDRE
(A Howard, K Chadwick. 1968)

Right of the main gully is a minor crag and splitting the centre of this is an obvious corner. At the bottom left of the diedre is a solitary pine tree almost hidden by the surrounding foliage. The route starts just above here and gives enjoyable and variable climbing on surprisingly good rock. 4–5 hours. 300m. Grade VI inf.

Scramble up left from the trees above the pine tree and onto a grass ledge beneath a square grey slab. Climb the centre of the slab (21m, 4°) to blocks on the top right. Ascend to the top of the blocks by a hanging crack on their left and continue via a leaning wall and a slab (45m, 5°). A chimney follows to the top right corner of the slabs where an exit is made into a diagonal crack on the vertical left side wall of the diedre. Follow

Blånebba 1,318m (4,323ft)

89. NORTH WEST RIDGE

An easy walk south along the ridge from Åndalsnes via Aksla (Route 75) and Mjølva (Route 79). 4km. About 3–4 hours. Grade I.

90. SOUTH EAST RIDGE

A pleasant scramble from Vengedal, especially if Holstind is included. About 3–4 hours. Grade II inf.

Follow the South Ridge of Holstind (Route 95) descending its North Ridge to the col. Scrambling and a little climbing (2°) lead to the summit of Blånebba.

91. SOUTH WALL
(R Høibakk, T Engvig)

An enjoyable climb on good steep rock; route finding is not obvious. 3–4 hours. 210m. Grade V.

From the col on the South East Ridge contour across to below the wall to a grass shelf beneath a steep slab grooved by black cracks (cairn). Start right up small gullies for 22m, then straight up by a groove for 7m to a gully slanting left and containing projecting flakes. Go a long way left before moving up and back right to the bottom of a distinct chimney. Ascend its left side to a spacious ledge beneath an overhanging wall. From the left end of the ledge climb a 9m chimney then up a gully towards the right until it overhangs. Exit round a corner to the right then 3m diagonally left up a steep slab to a small ledge. Start back right and up an overhanging section to a gully before traversing left to a small triangular shelf below a large overhang (peg). Move left round the corner and up the steep chimney to the top.

92. DESCENT BY THE NORTH WEST RIDGE

An easy walk along the broad crest of the ridge back to Åndalsnes. 2–3 hours.

93. DESCENT BY THE SOUTH EAST RIDGE

After initial scrambling (2°) an easy scree gully can be taken north east through crags to the foot of Vengedal Lake. 1–2 hours to seter.

Holstind 1,080m (3,542ft)

94. NORTH RIDGE

An easy scramble up from the col under the South East Ridge of Blånebba. Grade I.

95. SOUTH RIDGE

Usually used as the descent route for the ridge walk from Åndalsnes. The ascent is an easy walk up from Vengedal, either starting up the path that is used to approach the North Ridge of Romsdalshorn, or crossing the river just above the lake and scrambling up to the saddle of Lillefjell to join it near the pylons. The south ridge of Holstind is then an easy scramble. 2–3 hours from seter. Grade I.

96. SOUTH WEST PILLAR
(A Howard, B Tweedale. Winter 1967)

The west face is split by a great central couloir. To its right is the South West Pillar, the main obstacle to its ascent being the middle section which is climbed by shallow grooves well right of the obvious huge diedre. The lower third is a tediously vegetated introduction and the upper third is ridge scrambling. 10–12 hours. 1,000m. Grade V. Diags left and pg 62.

Start left of centre of the pillar and move left onto wooded slabs. Up these until forced right into a grassy gully after about 150m. After the gully (5°sup) zig-zag up slabs for

Blånebba
Holstind
Lillefjell
R96

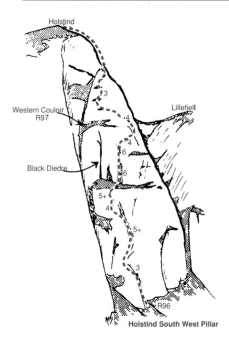

Holstind South West Pillar

Scramble up without real difficulty for 120–150m to slabs. Ascend these for a further three pitches (6°, 4°, 2°) to scree ledges below overhanging walls. The diedre is across to the right and is unclimbed.

Scramble up for a rope length to the bottom of steep broken slabs on the left of the couloir which are climbed for three pitches (5°sup, 4°) to a crack. Bridge up the crack to the top of a large flake and then traverse right into a corner (6°) using tension on a piton before moving up to a ledge. Continue up for almost 180m (4°, 5°, 3°) before moving right for a pitch to rejoin the couloir above the overhangs. The couloir is then followed up its right side for a pitch (5°) when 180m of easier rock (3°, 4°) leads to the final scramble up the South West Pillar.

98. DESCENT BY THE NORTH RIDGE

After descending the ridge to the col, a scree gully can be taken north east to the lower end of Vengedalsvatn. 1–2 hours to seter.

99. THE MJØLVA–BLÅNEBBA RIDGE
(First traverse unknown)

A pleasant ridge scramble with good views, 7–8 hours from Åndalsnes to Vengedal seter. Grade II inf.

Leave Åndalsnes by the wooden steps and follow the North West Ridge along the tops of Aksla, Mjølva and Blånebba without difficulty. Descend its South East Ridge to the col (2°) and scramble up to the top of Holstind. Descend its South Ridge, taking care in choice of route to avoid all difficulties, to the pylons on Lillefjell. Down the hillside to the road.

Romsdalshorn 1,555m (5,100ft)

100. NORTH FACE
(O H Furuseth, P Sabro, R Ødegard, H Nygard. 1920)

A classic route with some good climbing and fine situations high above the Romsdal valley. Perhaps the most popular climb in the area with a bolted 'abseil piste' for descent. The approach which takes about 1 hour

three pitches (4°, 5°sup, 3°) to a terrace with the diedre on the left.

Continue up two steep shallow diedres for 105m (6°) escaping with difficulty to another terrace. Traverse pleasantly rightwards across slabs for two pitches (3°) beneath an impending wall, then up a steep wall (4°) on good holds to a small platform. Move down right across a gully and up more slabs for 90m (3°, 4°) slowly trending left until the crest of the pillar is regained. Easy scrambling for 150m (2°) leads to a steeper section climbed in three rope lengths (3°) and the ridge is then followed easily to the summit.

97. WESTERN COULOIR
(D Little, K and R Stannard. 1967)

This is the couloir down the centre of the west face. Like the pillar, there is not much climbing of real merit. The route starts up the left of the couloir and keeps to this side for most of the way. There can be some danger from stonefall especially in the early season. Although the first ascent took 19 hours, a rope of two should complete the climb within 12 hours. 1,000m. Grade V. Diags pg 61 and above.

begins at a path which leaves the Vengedal road opposite the lowest part of the saddle well north of the North Face. Follow the path up to the col of Lillefjell (this is a popular short walk to this point, with stunning views of Romsdal and the Troll Wall as its reward). From the col, scramble pleasantly south and up the ridge to the gap under the north wall and the start of the climb. 2 hours. 300m. Grade III.

From the gap scramble easily up to the first steep section. This is best crossed from right to left (90m, 2°–3°) and leads to the scree platform at the bottom of the wall proper. The wall may be taken directly for 90m (4°) though it is often climbed by easier and more enjoyable pitches beginning from a groove on the left of the platform. After a pitch up the groove (3°), a steep wall is climbed on good holds (3°sup) to a square cut edge. Step out left and trend left up chimneys for two rope lengths. (3°, 2°) to scree ledges. Cross these, then slabs rightwards and ascend through a gap in the skyline (2°) onto the ridge. A further two rope lengths trending right (2°) bring one to the summit cairns.

Descent It was usual to descend via the Ordinary Route which is extremely long. Thanks to local guides there is now an abseil piste with 5 sets of chains back down the North Face, but it requires 50m double ropes. It starts from a hollow just below the top, 50m east of the finish of the North Face climb – you should have seen some or all of the chains on the way up.

An even quicker descent to Vengedal is being considered down the East Face which should also reduce possible stonefall and congestion on the North Face. Details will be put in the book in the summit hut.

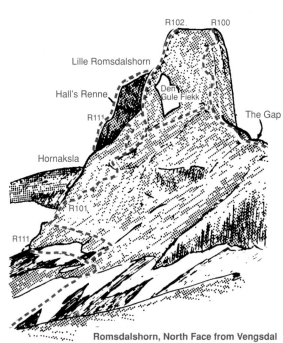

R102.   R100

Lille Romsdalshorn

Hall's Renne

Den Gule Flekk

R111

The Gap

Hornaksla

R101.

R111

Romsdalshorn, North Face from Vengsdal

101. ORDINARY ROUTE. SOUTH RIDGE VIA HALL'S RENNE
(C Hall, M Soggemoen, E Norahagen. 1881)

Rather a lot of scrambling on scree ledges, but an easy and still fairly popular route with very good rock on the final South Ridge. Probably the most nail-marked climb in Romsdal! 450m, most of which is easy scrambling. 3–4 hours from Hornvatn. Grade II. Diag above and pg 65.

From Hornvatn at the head of Vengedal go up the scree (or in early season, snow) slopes to below the east face of Romsdalshorn. A cairned path should then be evident leading leftwards between small crags to a step on the skyline. After a little climbing the path then continues its zig-zag course back rightwards to below a larger crag. This can be climbed directly (3°). The usual way avoids the obstacle by continuing rightwards with a little scrambling, then ascending a slab back left (2°). Further zig-zagging up the path, first towards the large, light coloured patch of rock on the east face (Den Gule Flekk), then back left with some climbing on slabs (2°), brings one into the huge gully splitting the peaks. This is Hall's Renne. Go easily up the gully on its right side (snow in the early season) to its steep exit wall which is climbed on its left to the col (2°sup). The steep south ridge then gives very enjoyable climbing on excellent holds (2°) to the summit.

102. EAST RIDGE
(H Berg, A R Heen, O Roed. 1947)

The route branches right from the Ordinary Route at the point where it goes left towards slabs leading to Hall's Renne. A fairly steep line but not much really good climbing. 4 hours from Hornvatn. 180m. Grade IV. Diag pg 63.

From the path of the Ordinary Route traverse

up right on for one pitch towards Den Gule Flekk (the light patch of rock) and move back left onto the steep curving ridge on its left edge. This is then followed to the summit, past a steep wall finishing in a gently sloping gully.

It is also possible to continue the ascending rightwards traverse beneath Den Gule Flekk and out onto the scree platform on the North Face.

103. WEST WALL DIRECT
(B Halvorsen, O Eliassen, J Teigland, O D Enersen. 1965)

A steep and serious climb on doubtful rock, in a fine situation high above the valley. The time for the first ascent was 16 hours with a

The Trolltindler from Lillefjell above Vengedal

bivouac at halfway. A rope of two should complete the climb in one day from Vengedal. 300m. Grade V sup.

Start near red-yellow rocks left of The Cross and about 75m right of the north face. Climb three pitches (4°sup, 4°, 3°sup) straight up to a belay on the edge of a white slab. Move out right and after about 12m climb up to a peg belay (5°sup). Continue upwards and then right to a large shelf (5°).(Bivouac, first ascent.) From the right end of the ledge climb up for about 20m (4°) and then trend right with difficulty (5°sup) and step down to a belay on a good ledge above the cross. From this ledge traverse about 9m right and then up. After a 5m layback (6°inf) move out right again and up a short slab and exit right (difficult). Now follow the natural formation rightwards for 1½ rope lengths (2°). Ascend a difficult groove (5°) trending left, then right, for another pitch (4°). The next two pitches (2°) lead pleasantly to the top.

104. WEST WALL CROSS CLIMB
(O Enersen, J Teigland. 1966)

A steep and impressive climb on doubtful rock, comparable with the Direct Route. Mostly 4° and 5° with some 5°sup and 6°inf. 8 hours. Grade V sup.

Start about 40m right of the Direct, and ascend towards The Cross for a rope length to a shallow groove. From the top of the groove make an airy traverse right to big hanging blocks. Move up again to a small ledge and trend left in an exposed position, crossing the Direct Route beneath the (6°inf) pitch. Continue left to a gully which is climbed for two rope lengths. Exit rightwards and ascend three pitches to the top.

105. WEST WALL, ORIGINAL ROUTE
(R Høibakk, F Hortnagl, A Mayr. 1959)

A steep but somewhat artificial line with some interesting climbing and good situations. Once above halfway, escape is possible from all pitches by moving into the gully leading to the south col. The lower half is, however, inescapable and could be difficult after rain. 3–4 hours. 300m. Grade IV sup.

Gain the foot of the west wall as in Route 103, and contour round to a point between The Cross and the prominent black gully. Move diagonally up the left side of the gully for two rope lengths (3°, 5°) on narrow slabs to a cave on the left. Traverse right with difficulty (5°sup) and up to ledges. Bear rightwards across easy angled slabs and exit round the skyline into the main gully, 'Gjelet',

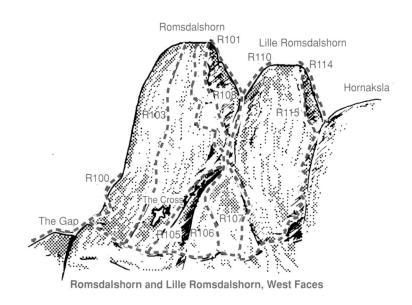

Romsdalshorn and Lille Romsdalshorn, West Faces

move up a few feet, then back left into a smaller, hidden gully (3°). Follow this to a shelf, then straight out left onto the West Wall on excellent rock and across to a square block in a fine situation. Directly up to large ledges (3°sup.) then left to blocks and straight up again (5°) for another rope length, exiting by a steep crack (3°) to the summit, almost opposite the hut.

106. NASEN AND GJELET
(R and S N Meyer. 1939)

Follows a line up the protruding buttress (Nasen) right of the previous route, to the gully leading to the col between Romsdalshorn and Lille Romsdalshorn. The lower buttress leading up to the gully has some interesting pitches on fairly steep rock. 2–4 hours. 300m. Grade IV. Diag pg 65.

From ledges beneath The Cross, traverse rightwards for two rope lengths, passing the previous route and gaining the buttress on its right. Move up for a short pitch, then trend leftwards for about 60m onto the ridge above the upper edge of the black gully in Route 105. A steep 15m slab follows to a good ledge, escaping left under an overhang and up to a hollow at the foot of the main gully. This is followed without difficulty to the col and the South Ridge climbed to the summit.

107. BY ALTANEN AND GJELET
(E Fjeld, S Suhrke. 1928)

The original, and easiest way of approaching the upper gully. The route follows the right-hand side of the buttress previously mentioned. 2–3 hours. 300m. Grade IV inf. Diag pg 65.

Approach the buttress as in Route 106, but continue horizontally right for a third rope length to a small crag, then diagonally up right across steep rock to the obvious platform. This is Altanen. Continue up rightwards to reach the ill-defined gully which is climbed by a difficult pitch. Traverse right along a gallery to gain a steep gully which leads to large ledges, left of which is the main gully leading to the col. The South Ridge leads to the top.

All the three preceding routes can be reached directly from Romsdal by extremely tedious zig-zagging up the steep hillside. It is mostly vegetation – NOT RECOMMENDED!

The upper sections of these routes, from their junction in the main gully are all interchangeable. There is a fourth independent finish, namely:

108. SOUTH WEST RIDGE
(A R Heen, P Harvold. 1957)

An indefinite line affording numerous variations. The rock is steep and the holds are good if a little suspect. 120m. Grade III.

The ridge is the vague junction of the West Wall with the upper part of the main gully. It can be reached by descending from the col or from any of the previous three routes, as an alternative finish. From the gully, climb as directly as possible up the ridge, keeping just on the west wall to avoid any difficulties.

109. DESCENT BY THE ORDINARY ROUTE

Climb down the South Ridge (2°) to the col, or reach it by 2 abseils from slings. Now, abseil into Hall's Renne from a peg in place 3m to the right, looking out. (Actually, it's not a peg its a bent gun barrel fixed there by Arne Randers Heen!) Now follow the path down the left side of the gully (snow in early season). DO NOT continue all the way down Hall's Renne. After 90m or so, the path trends left out of the gully and zig-zags down slabby rock on the east face, then left and right between steeper rocks where another of Arne Randers' bent gun barrel abseil points will be found. Make a 45m abseil and continue down to scree (or snow) slopes in the upper corrie. Go left (north) along its top edge to reach the scree or snow slopes which lead down to Hornvatn and Vengedal. 2 hours.

Lille Romsdalshorn
1,525m (5,002ft)

110. ORDINARY ROUTE, NORTH RIDGE
(C Hall, M Soggemoen. 1884)

The route starts from the Kløfta or col above

Hall's Renne and is seldom used except in descent. 1–3 hours from the foot of the East Face. Grade II. Diag pg 65.

Follow the Romsdalshorn Ordinary Route up to Kløfta then ascend the North Ridge for 90m (2°) to the top.

111. EAST RIDGE
(R Høibakk, D Dawes. 1958)

A fairly direct route with pleasant climbing. 2–4 hours. 360m. Grade IV. Diag pg 63.

Walk up from Vengedal to the glacier in the corrie under the east face (Route 62). Start the climb by scrambling easily upwards (1°) for three rope lengths to the beginning of the difficulties. The ridge is then followed for two pitches to a big grass shelf which is traversed for 27m left. After a further three rope lengths straight up, the angle eases to the summit.

112. EAST FACE – RAF ROUTE
(R Appleyard, R Betteridge. July 1978)

500m. Grade IV

Start as for Route 111 up easy ledges, then follow a groove slanting left. After about 50m, when below a prominent square overhang, leave groove on right and follow easy slab to belay on ledges (70m). Now, instead of going up left as for the East Ridge route, traverse easily down and right, to cross the foot of Hall's Renne then up easy ledges to below a steep wall (50m). Straight up a cracked wall – good rock (crux). After 20m step round right into a groove and follow to small ledge with good belays (35m). Up over blocks on right, then trend back left and up steep exposed rock, passing a large balanced pillar 50m. Easy ground, trending left for (70m) to a point overlooking Hall's Renne. Traverse left on steep rock, and climb a difficult exposed section passing below small overhang (35m). Belay in Hall's Renne. Follow Hall's Renne for 20m then traverse left (50m). Continue the traverse, up and left to join the East Ridge route at top of a very exposed wall (50m). Follow ridge up a very steep, exposed section to easy ground (30m). Scramble to summit.

113. SOUTH EAST WALL
(B Halvorsen, T Engvig. 1963)

A fairly steep climb. 3–5 hours. 180m. Grade V inf.

From the snowfields under the East Face scramble up the diagonal gully which leads to the south col of Lille. Before reaching the col it is possible to move up onto the steep wall and follow a line trending diagonally left to the top. (Some difficult pitches.)

114. SOUTH RIDGE
(A Danish party. 1956)

A short but natural line with a long approach. 3–5 hours from Vengedal. 120m. Grade V inf. Diag pg 65.

From the glacier in the eastern corrie, ascend the left flank of the diagonal gully to the col, then straight up the South Ridge on good steep rock to the summit. Pegs are required for the first pitch, and a 3m high barrier wall at 60m provides a problem.

115. SOUTH WEST WALL
(A R Heen. 1929)

An inaccessible little climb. Approach is possible either from the col of the previous route or via Altanen (Route 107) on Romsdalshorn's West Face. The climb begins10m down from the col. 120m. Grade III sup. Diag pg 65.

Ascend a 3m groove, then easier for 8m to a ledge. An awkward pitch follows, up and left before traversing rightwards to reach the south ridge where it eases off to the summit.

Hornaksla Lower West Face (Roadside Crag)

This is the lower part of Hornaksla about 400m from the Troll Wall viewing place and car park and almost opposite the Trollryggen Pillar. It is a popular and easily accessible steep crag, which now has over 60 modern routes, with grades mostly between Norwegian 5+ and 8. See *Klatring i Romsdal*. Descents are by abseil from bolts.

Two of the earliest climbs on the crag were originally followed all the way to the summit:

116. JUGOSLAVIAN ROUTE
(1970)

No details, but straight up the nose of the crag and continue to the top.

117. SOUTH WEST SPUR
(A Wilmott, M J Spring, D Edwards, A Heppenstall. 1969)

Superb slab climbing in its lower half. This was the first route to be opened on this now famous roadside cliff. Unfortunately, for those who continue, it deteriorates into exhausting scrambling higher up.

The spur drops down from the right-hand end of the level shoulder, its base forming a steep 350m wall reaching almost to the roadside. Running up the left side of this wall is a slabby white ramp, easily identified by a telegraph pole at its foot. The climb starts by the stream about 20m right of the pole and about ten minutes from the road. Approx 10 hours. 1,950m. Grade V.

Climb up more or less following the stream which descends the slabs for 120m to a slabby terrace (4°, 3°). Move right for 30m then go up and left through vegetation for approx. 45m to regain the slabs again at the earliest opportunity. Move left along a slabby terrace below steeper rock for 12m to a position just right of the stream. Climb up left to the stream and up it for 3m. Move left round the arête into a shallow corner. Up this and belay below a wide crack (45m, 6°). Continue up to an easing in the angle after 21m. Move up left then back right to belay by a big spike (45m, 5°).

Continue in the same line for two rope lengths (5°,4°), then up the slabs more easily for several hundred feet until the ramp becomes horizontal ledges. (Mainly 2° with pitches of 3° and a pitch of 5°). Follow the ledges leftwards for 60m to a small cairn. Go more or less straight up for 45m (3°) then with greater difficulty (45m, 5°) until it is possible to trend easily rightwards (45m, 2°) to a scree ledge with a huge protruding block. Climb the cracks above for 18m and move left by overhangs. Continue to a good stance (37m, 4°). Move easily left then right to below steeper rock (37m, 2°). Zig-zag upwards for 45m (6°) then easily up right to a huge terrace.

Follow this easily up right and around the skyline. Continue upwards (odd short pitches of 3°) to below the final steep tower of rock. Easily up left almost until the ramp peters out, then up an odious wet chimney (30m, 5°). Move right then left for 60m (2°)

to a boulder field. Up this and take the last rock strip more or less in its centre (60m, 3°) to finish on the ridge.

DESCENT FROM HORNAKSLA SUMMIT

From snow patches behind the ridge, go down to meet the Romsdalshorn descent on the left (west) side of the corrie. Follow the path down. 3 hours.

Now, back to the roadside crag:

118. INGRID ESPELID
(K Svanemyr, B Østigard. 1978)

This is a big diedre which can be seen from the road at the left end of the lower tier. Three interesting rope lengths. 120m. Grade 5°inf.

Descent Easy return to the right down the ramp.

119. GRAVRAMMER
(H Doseth, R Amundsen. 1978)

Originally climbed with some aid by A Willmott and E Ward Drummond in August 1970. It follows the big crack which starts from the cave and goes up the centre of this impressive wall towards the big roofs in the final tier, which are now climbed by Super Crack. Nine rope lengths on good rock. 400m. Norwegian Grade 6+.

Start up a diedre (4°) leading up to the cave (30m). Climb the right wall of the cave (5°sup) and continue up the big crack chimney (4°sup) 40m. Continue up the crack and over some vegetated ground right to the start of a black chimney (4° and 2°). Up this to the first big ramp (4°, 4°sup, 5°) 30m. Go over it leftwards and start on the right wall of a steep diedre (6°). Continue up this and an overhanging 'off-width' crack (6°) above, 30m. Continue up a diedre (5°sup) and take a beautiful crack going leftwards (5°) to a sloping ledge, 30m. Traverse 5m left and up a steep crack (4°sup) and up the gully above (3°) 25m. Now up the steep, ugly looking gully above following it leftwards (5°, 4°, 6°inf), 30m. Then up and out of the narrow

gully (4°sup) and up easier ground to the second big ramp.

Descent Follow the ramp easily down without abseils. It is possible to continue up some cracks 50m to the left and even to the top of Hornaksla if desired. Or, continue up the final pitches of Super Crack with a little aid required.

120. SUPER CRACK (GRAVRAMMER HEAD WALL)
(Jan van der Muelen and Christoph von Schultz. 1985)

This takes the diedres and roofs directly above Gravrammer for four rope lengths. Norwegian 7, A1. Diag pg 68.

The first 40m pitch is the crux followed by 50m (6-) up the next corner, moving right (7-) to belay. Up and right again for 30m (A1, then 4+) and a pitch of 4+ to finish.

In addition to the steep approaches from Hornaksla Crag, the summit of Hornaksla can be reached by more traditional ways, both from Vengedal and from Romsdal.

Hornaksla 1,515m (4,969ft)

121. EAST RIDGE
(Party unknown)

Taking the Ordinary Route from Vengedal to Romsdalshorn, this shoulder, which is south of Lille Romsdalshorn, can be approached easily by scrambling up from the glacier in the corrie beneath its east side. It can be incorporated in the approach to the south ridge of Lille Romsdalshorn. 4–5 hours from seter. Grade I.

122. EAST FACE AND COULOIR
(Soldan and Zahoransky. Winter, 12–13 Mar 1974)

No details available.

123. WEST FACE
(A R Heen and party)

Ascend from Romsdal by a long and tedious

Ole Haltvick on the descent ramp from Hornaksla cliff

vegetated scramble up the west face. Above the tree line, the route takes the prominent scree ramp rightwards to the skyline. From here a long scree ledge is taken back left and a little scrambling remains to the top. NOT RECOMMENDED. 8 hours. Grade II.

124. SOUTH WEST SLABS
(First ascent unknown)

The route follows the great ramp of slabs from Horgheim in Romsdal. It involves very little actual climbing but the rock scenery is excellent. Approx 10 hours. 1,800m. Grade IV. Photo pg 68.

Follow the upper ramp of slabs, taking the easiest line. A 50m wall at three-quarters height provides the only real obstacle (5°). Bear left beyond this (loose) to a notch in the skyline and ascend steep rocks on good holds to the summit.

Descent From snow patches behind the ridge, go down to meet the Romsdalshorn descent on the left (west) side of the corrie. Follow the path down into Vengedal. 3 hours

Olaskartind 1,428m (4,644ft)

This is the next top south of Hornaksla.

125. WEST RIDGE
(A R Heen and party. 1929)

Approach as Route 121 to the col from which the West Ridge leads without difficulty to the pyramid-like summit. 4–5 hours from Vengedal. Grade I.

The north and south ridges may also be climbed easily, the latter from Olaskarvatn to the east.

Kalskratind 1,797m (5,891ft)

125. NORTH WEST RIDGE
(L Broch and party. 1865)

A long approach with no difficulties and no real merit. It is the usual descent route. 4–5 hours from Hornvatn. Grade I.

Using Route 62, walk up to Olaskar Lake and then south east across the plateau (snow) to the rounded ridge which gives scrambling to the north summit. A sharper, pinnacled ridge curves south east from here to the higher south summit. To the left is the hanging 'Uncharted Glacier' (see below) high on its north east face, whilst on the right is the vast and complex system of walls and ridges forming the South West Face .

127. THE UNCHARTED GLACIER
(R Appleyard, B Betteridge, P Horth. July 1978)

The 'uncharted glacier' mentioned in the previous route. The first ascent took 6 hrs. Grade III

Approach is from the eastern end of lake Svartvatnet, and then an easy scramble up through scree and past small rock faces and snowfields to the foot of the glacier, at its right-hand (west) side.

Go 30m up easy snow slopes to the foot of a dirty ice field, rock belay, then up the ice field to a rock wall. Bypass this on its left and ascend to belay on rock as a snowfield starts (100m). Straight up on steep, firm snow to peg belay on an overhanging rock wall (50m). Now, move left and up, keeping close to the rock wall, and climb snow to crevassed

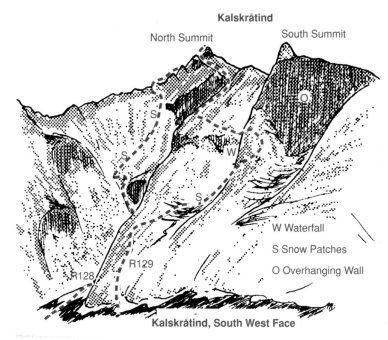

Kalskråtind

North Summit   South Summit

W Waterfall

S Snow Patches

O Overhanging Wall

R129

R128

Kalskråtind, South West Face

section. On first ascent, this was passed by a snow bridge, followed by a 5m vertical ice wall. Traverse back right to rock belay (100m). From here, go up right on hard water-ice to higher snowfields. Rock belay on right (50m), then steep but good snow is followed until it is possible to climb a short gully on the right onto the broad rock ridge (70m) and so to the top.

Now we come to the big routes climbing up from the depths of Romsdal:

128. SOUTH WEST COULOIR
(G Clark, F Yeoman, J Cooper, R Baldwin. 1967)

Better climbing than the South West Buttress. The route begins in the obvious gully line running up the west face, and keeps up its left side to the north summit. A long, therefore serious climb in impressive surroundings. The lower section could be impassable after wet weather. About 12 hours. 1,500m. Grade V inf.

Approach easily from the Romsdal road near Marstein Station and follow the gully bed

into the amphitheatre. Take the obvious line up its left side (a waterfall is seen directly above) and continue straight up for about 180m (4°sup, 6°inf, 4°, 3°) to below a second small waterfall. Trend right across a slab then up a wet slab and groove (4°) to a large platform below a waterfall and very steep walls.

Escape by traversing left, down a little and across slabs for 90m to easy ground, then upwards to snow patches near the upper section of the couloir. Follow the gully line roughly to another snow patch (mostly 3°) and continue for three rope lengths to below steep white walls. The next pitch goes right then left to a wet slab beneath overhanging walls. This is climbed on the left (4°,1 peg). Then trend leftwards (5°) to reach easy ground below the final walls. Traverse left from a rock spike to the foot of a V-groove and up the slab on the left to finish in a small chimney-groove (5°sup). Scrambling now leads up the ridge to the top. The difficult upper section of this route could probably be avoided by traversing out left onto the ridge from a point above the upper snowfield.

129. SOUTH WEST BUTTRESS
(O D Enersen, J Teigland. 1964)

Right of the above couloir, a buttress runs up the face to a point between the two summits. Halfway up, on its right is a waterfall. The route winds its way up this buttress, finishing on the north summit. The climb contains no really great difficulties but is nevertheless serious especially after wet weather and gives an unforgettable impression of rock savagery of unaccustomed dimensions. Route finding is not easy. 15 hours. Over 1,800m. Grade IV sup.

Ascend the buttress which is covered with dwarf birch trees, keeping left of a stream to a steep slab (4°). Continue by the easiest line which leads to a steep wet gully (4°), and then on in the direction of the waterfall to a snow patch near the stream. (Good bivouac place, 6–8 hours from start.)

Traverse right and follow a gully to slabs leading to the foot of the waterfall. The vast overhanging white wall is on the right. Up one pitch and traverse right on steep rock then diagonally left for two or three pitches over ledges to a corner. Continue up slabs for about 60m until it is possible to descend to, and cross, the stream. One is now back on the original buttress, and the south summit is up to the right, the north summit to the left.

Ascend leftwards up the buttress towards the summit walls, then left beneath them up steep steps (3°) to a snow patch. Continue by slabs and gullies (3°, 4°) leftwards to the gap in the ridge south of the north summit and up the ridge to finish.

130. DESCENT BY THE NORTH WEST RIDGE

Scramble down the ridge then north west to Olaskarvatn and down Route 62 to Vengedal. 4–5 hours.

131. MONGE FOSSEN
(A Gruner, M Haugen, B ,Østigard, Ø Spjelkavik, O Stavrand, H Doseth)

This is one of Romsdal's most beautiful waterfalls, though now it is only allowed to run free during the month of July, otherwise it can be snuff-dry slabs. This is because its source has been diverted into the hydroelectric system. 700m. 6 hours, Grade IV.

The start is from Romsdal 100m past Monge Farm following the dried out stream. Easy scrambling to reach the first big terrace. From there the route follows the right diedre of the slabs (3°). From the second terrace it continues up the diedres with a difficult move near the top (5°inf), then it goes left and right again over easy slabs to the top.

Beyond here is one of Romsdal's biggest and most imposing walls, with some multi-day routes:

Mongejura 1,276m (4,185ft)

132. SOUTH WALL
(B Thompson, J Stanger, D Walsh. 1967)

A long and serious route with some excellent climbing, tackling the great wall behind the church at Monge in Romsdal. After traversing in from the left the route goes up the centre of the face and finishes abruptly with a pitch of artificial work. All water must be carried and a selection of pegs including several thin blades, bugaboos and three or four wedges or bongs. Bivouac ledges are adequate. 3 days. 1,200m. Grade VI.

A line of grassy terraces leads from the left side of the face to the great central bay. Gain the terraces by a steep slab (60m, 5°) and a crack (15m, A1, 4 wedges). Follow the terraces rightwards for 180m to grey slabs in the centre of the face. These are climbed for 150m (4°sup, 5°) to a large terrace. A prominent grassy rake now rises steeply to the right and is followed for 90m (5°) to a black chimney.

After the chimney (15m, 5°, 3 pegs), traverse the steep wall on the right to a small stance (30m, 5°sup, 1 peg). Continue up to the right to a steep groove which is climbed to a good ledge (45m, 5°). First bivouac.

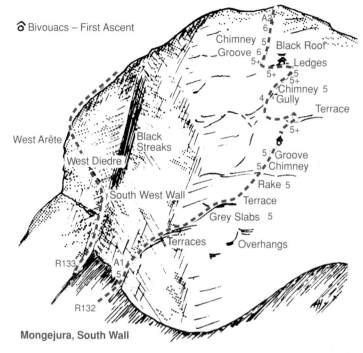

ô Bivouacs – First Ascent

Mongejura, South Wall

Climb the corner on the left (2 pegs) then traverse down right across the steep wall to the continuation of the grass rake (45m 5°sup). Follow the rake to slabby ledges (45m, 4°sup, 5°) and continue easily for 30m to the second large terrace. Traverse easily left for 60m until a difficult traverse (5°sup) can be made to a steep gully which is climbed for 60m (4°) to a fine ledge beneath a steep vegetated corner.

Ascend the corner and the chimney above to a large sloping ledge (36m, 5°) above which there is easier climbing (2°sup, 3°) up a system of cracks and ledges for a rope length leading to a series of short grooves. These are climbed moving left and back right to more grass ledges (39m 5°sup). Step down across the gully on the right from which easy scrambling leads to a short steep wall (3m, 5°). Traverse left above this on slabs for 45m to a small bay beneath a large black roof and then easily right on broken rock to a grassy corner. Step right, and up steep loose rock to a good ledge (45m, 4°sup), then a steep groove (6m 5°) to easier ground and a huge

ledge beneath a prominent black overhang. Fine site for second bivouac on left in a small cave.

From the bivouac traverse left with difficulty for 39m (5°sup). Peg in place to assist the last man on the traverse. Continue by ascending traverse right up a steep rake, then follow steep grass to a small belay ledge (39m 5°sup). Traverse right, then straight up to a steep greasy groove leading to a small bay (45m 5°, 6°). Right again to the small overhanging groove (5°) then along easier ledges and steep grass to the next little bay. Continue right, then up to the top of a pedestal (38m 5°), above which is a pitch up a steep groove and a very loose chimney to a huge detached flake (5°). The wall behind the flake is climbed direct for 39m (5°sup, 6°) to a slabby ledge beneath the final yellow wall. Finish by thin flake cracks of doubtful stability which are pegged to the left side of the roof. With pegs between the roof and the wall, traverse right to the exit chimney which leads abruptly to the top (24m A2, 16 pegs, 1 wedge).

133. WEST DIEDRE
(J Stanger, B Thompson, M Burte. 1968)

A steep and sustained climb, the main difficulties being artificial work high on the wall. The first ascent took three days. Water must be carried on the actual climb for all bivouacs. 1,050m, with 600m of actual climbing. Grade VI. Diag pg 73.

Approach from Romsdal road directly below the overhanging arête and up through very steep forest for 2½ hours to a 90m rock step. Climb this (loose, 4°, 4°sup) to the forested ledge beneath the diedre, and the start of the climb proper. Excellent bivouac with water at the back of the diedre.

The next few pitches are loose and vegetated and start on the left on easy angled rock fanning out from the back of the diedre. A rope length up slabs (3°) and a short corner (4°, 3°) lead to a good ledge, the next pitch ascending via jammed block (4°) to a steep

wall on the left (5°) above which a swing right (5°sup) is made into a steep corner (5°) which leads to a stance and thread belay. Now, following what appears to be the easiest way, climb a steep slab (4°) to a tree at 15m then a short wall on the left (4°) before traversing right (3°) to a clean cut corner, ('The 10m Corner'). Climb this (A1, 5°) and traverse right to a good stance and pinnacle belay beneath an overhanging crack. The wide corner crack is followed (A1, bongs, 5°) and the corner above (5°sup) to a good stance beyond which a steep slab on the left (4°sup) leads to a grassy ledge. (First bivouac site – poor.)

Ascend the corner on the right (4°sup), then the corner crack (loose, A2, A3, bongs) to a small roof. Pass this on the left, then climb the corner and slab above (5°sup) to belay on a large perched block. Now go diagonally up the steep slab (4°) to a good stance and good bivouac site, then ascend a few feet to

The Trolltinder from Lillefjell, below Romsdalhorn's North Wall

a crack and go round a corner for a few feet (3°, 4°). Go straight up from here on easier angled rock (4°) to perched blocks, then semi-hand traverse across the wall on the left (5°) and continue easily to grass ledges (3°). Climb grass and rock (3°) to a block belay at the start of a very obvious traverse line across the wall on the left. Follow the traverse for 36m towards the arête (5°, 5°sup, 4°) then slabs for a further 12m (4°) to a grassy bay – a magnificent pitch, difficult to reverse. A steep corner follows (9m 5°) above which go easily along a grassy terrace for 30m to a big block below a huge detached flake. (Second bivouac – good site.)

Squeeze behind the flake and make a short and sensational traverse to a diedre on the edge of the arête and climb this (A1, 5°) to ledges. Continue in the diedre for 18m (5°) to a huge platform beneath an overhanging wall. The following pitch is the crux of the climb and required two attempts on the first ascent. Climb the obvious crack (A1, A2) until it becomes vague, then proceed on knife blades and bolts (A3, A4) until it Is possible to free climb to a good platform on the arête (5°sup), (10 bolts and 4 or 5 pegs left in place). Now traverse easily left, then climb the broken wall above to a steep corner of jammed blocks (4°, 5°) leading to a grassy bay. Take the corner on the left of this and traverse left round a corner then across a slab using undercut holds and up to easier ground (5°, 4°), a superb pitch.

Mixed scrambling over grass and rock outcrops for a further 450m bring one to the top where water is available in small lakes.

134. THE SOUTH PILLAR
(H C Doseth, A Lundahl. 1981)

One of Norway's best big wall climbs. See Klatring i Romsdal which also has the topo. Grade VI.

135. DESCENT BY THE NORTH SHOULDER

Walk for 3km over easy ground on the northern side to the col between this peak

and Kalskratind. From here an extremely long scree gully cuts down the western hillside into Romsdal. 4–5 hours.

Before concluding this area, there is one other excellent expedition which deserves mention.

136. THE VENGETIND–KVANDALSTIND–ROMSDALSHORN HORSESHOE
(R Høibakk and party)

This magnificent mountain tour includes all the best ridges and peaks in the Vengetind and Romsdalshorn Groups. The expedition can be made in either direction round the horseshoe though the first girdle was anti-clockwise and included a major climb on each peak. Should these be avoided, the trip would still be extremely worthwhile and would then be II sup. The following notes describe the kind of route taken on the first traverse. 3 days. Grade V.

Starting from Vengedal, ascend to the summit of Store Vengetind by the West Ridge (IV inf.) Descend to the 'skar' down the Gallery on the East Face (II) and continue up the north Ridge to the summit of Lille Vengetind (II). Descend by the South Ridge to the col (II), and regain the summit by the South West Wall (IV). Descend again and follow the ridge along to the summit of Søre Vengetind, and down to the col under the West Ridge of Kvandalstind. Ascend this (III inf) to the summit, including Torshammer Pinnacle (III inf). Descend by the South Face (II sup) and cross the plateau past Olaskar Lake to the foot of Romsdalshorn East Face.

Ascend to Lille Romsdalshorn by the East Ridge (IV), then down the north ridge (II) to the 'Klofta'. Up to the summit of Romsdalshorn by the South Ridge (II), and descend the North Face by abseil to Lillefjell. Cross Lillefjell and ascend the South Ridge of Holstind, descending by its North Ridge to the col under Blånebba which is climbed by its South Wall (V). The ridge is then followed northwards, over Mjølva to Nesaksla whose North West Ridge brings one into Åndalsnes.

The Trolltind Group

Romsdal's 'Three Pillars', Breitind, Søndae Trolltind and Trollryggen, with Hornaksla cliff on the right

The Trolltinder are a fierce and famous ridge of peaks forming the western flank of the Romsdal valley to which they present an unbroken barrier of rock of 8km in length and about 1.5km in height. Most of this is a vast area of glaciated slabs sweeping up into the vertical. To the south are the Three Pillars, three great ridges supporting the summits of Breitind, Søndre Trolltind (Semletind) and Trollryggen. Above the huge scree-filled corrie right of the last named is the north facing Trolltind Wall – Trollveggen, the largest vertical rock wall in Europe – a major attraction for tourists and big-wall climbers although, since 1998, parts of it have been seriously damaged by massive rock falls.

On their western side, the Trolltinder lose much of their savagery and present a more friendly face to the Isterdal valley. On this side, the dominant faces are the West Face of Stighorn and the West and South pillars of Store Trolltind which are difficult of access. The majority of the easier routes and descents are therefore on the western side of the range, mostly via Trollstig, or Sogge.

These two valleys are home to some of the longest and most serious rock climbs in Europe. Additionally, Isterdal is famous for the magnificent Stigfoss waterfall through which the road winds its tortuous way in and out of the 'box canyon'. Here also is the old pack horse trail 'Kløvstien' from Valldal, which is well worth following as is the delightful trek from near the top of the Trollstig Falls through Langfjelldalen to Vermedalen in Romsdal. Finally, Romsdal is also renowned for its salmon fishing river, once one of the best in Norway. Sadly considerable problems have been experienced with diseases carried into it, probably from salmon farms out at sea but the river has been opened for fishing again in recent years.

Bus services run up both the Isterdal and Romsdal valleys. Also, as has been mentioned, there are numerous campsites in both Isterdal or Romsdal. Fiva Farm is the nearest one can get by car to the Troll Wall area and is about 10km from Åndalsnes by road. Camping is possible in the birch woods below the wall (ask at Fiva).

Up in the mountains there are a number of bivouacs. The best is the well constructed little hut on the summit of Store Trolltind. This is ideal for two, but can hold more of course. At the foot of the western side of the pinnacle of Klumpen there is a small overhang which gives some shelter and is occasionally used as a bivouac though little more than 1km to the south west is a much better site. Here, in the boulder moraine on the south east rim of Stogrovbotnen and only a few metres west of the main path is a large cairned boulder with a well sheltered (though frequently damp) bivouac beneath it. One kilometre south west again, and by the side of the path to Trollstigen, is another similar bivouac though this is often concealed by snow until late August.

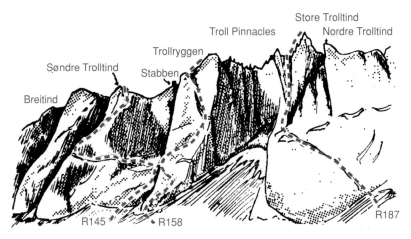

The Trolltinder, Southern and Central Peaks from Romsdal

Walks between Isterdal and Romsdal

137. ALNESDALEN

The southern end of the main peaks of the group is defined by the valley of Alnesdalen, which leads from Alnes Lake, just below the road north of the actual Trollstig pass, to the edge of the steep hillside above Marstein Station in Romsdal. A pleasant walk has been reported here, of 7km (often with much snow in the early season). It is possible to descend into Romsdal without difficulty if care is taken, or to contour south east above Romsdal and join the path in Vermedal. The summit of Breitind to the north is also accessible from here.

138. LANGFJELLDAL–VERMEDAL

This is a well known and worthwhile fell walk, usually done from west to east (more down than up!). The total distance is about 24km.

Leave the Valldal road about 1.5km beyond the Trollstig pass, and follow Langfjelldal (long mountain valley) roughly south east until it leads over a pass with a lake, often frozen, into Vermedal. This valley, which is of a similar length, descends through some beautiful ancient woodland with old seters and past the impressive Verma Falls into Verma at the head of Romsdal.

Now for bigger and steeper things:

Breitind 1,759m (5,770ft)

139. WEST RIDGE
(O K Lyngheim, Soeyer Brothers. 1880)

Seldom used except in descent. 3 hours, Grade I.

Follow the path up from the top of Stigfoss (Route 182) until at the top of the second hillside (cairns). The West Ridge is now on the right (east) and can be followed to the summit without difficulty.

140. SOUTH EAST RIDGE
(Jiskor and Zahoransky. February 1976)

A winter ascent. No details.

141. EASTERN COULOIR
(A R Heen, O D Enersen, J Teigland, P Svendsaas. 1964)

The climb starts in Romsdal from snowfields at the foot of the great South East Gully marking the left edge of the South East Face. It follows the obvious ramp rightwards then ascends the couloir in the centre of the face to a snowfield. It then zig-zags to the top, passing through a waterfall. This makes the route difficult of exit after prolonged rain, especially so since the crux is high up. A good mountaineering route – route finding is not obvious and for its grade (mostly 3°) it is a fairly serious undertaking. 8–9 hours. About 1,500 m. Grade IV.

From Horgheim in Romsdal, a bridge crosses the river and an easy walk follows to the foot of the South East Gully. The route begins up a long ramp leading rightwards towards the crest of the East Pillar (some snow, especially early in the season). Just before reaching a long and large permanent snow slope on the upper half of the ramp, the climb moves left to gain the South East Face.

A rope length up a slab, then a few pitches back right lead to scree at the foot of the couloir. Now, move left and go directly up the face (5°, the Enersen-Teigland Variant) or take the natural and easier line up the left ridge of the couloir for three pitches. Traverse 45m back into it at the end, and then another three rope lengths up left again to an outstanding block. The Variant joins the route again here.

Continue leftwards up the line of the couloir, finishing by a small slab to a snow patch beneath the summit walls. From here move

rightwards over slabs (5°) to a good stance. Traverse right for another rope length then up the obvious leftward depression for three pitches to the summit.

142. EAST PILLAR
(A Howard, B Tweedale. 1967)

One of the famous 'Three Pillars of Romsdal'. The route follows the pillar more or less directly and can be divided into three sections. The first is very obvious – the great winding chimney which gives 750m of excellent climbing on good rock; full of interest and variety. Next, the route follows easy grassy breaks up the right side of the pillar till beneath the summit towers which provide the final third and are again taken on the right. A

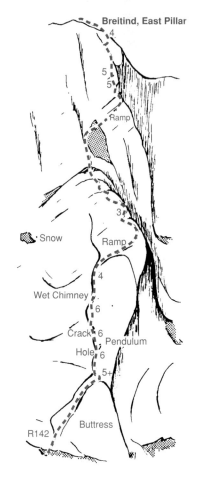

long and recommendable mountaineering route; the initial chimneys could be much more difficult in the early season or after wet weather. 10–12 hours. Over 2,000m of climbing. Grade V. Photo above.

The quickest approach is to cross the bridge from Horgheim and drive, or walk, up the rough track to the farm at Lyngheim. It is then an easy walk through the trees to the foot of the pillar.

Solo easily up the couloir and chimney which forms the left edge of the supporting buttress for about 200m (2°), to its top from which follow a groove for a rope length (3°). A diagonal descent left (3°) and a small wall (5°sup) gains re-entry to the chimney which is followed for about 120m (4°,1°) to below the first apparent impasse: a massive overhang. Climb up (4°) and walk through a hole beneath it and up to a belay on the right-hand wall.

Progress up the chimney is now most definitely barred, this time by a wet green overhang above a smooth wall. It is avoided by ascending a very steep groove on the right for about 18m to a small doubtful spike

from which a long diagonal tension traverse is made back down to the bed of the chimney (6°). After a pitch up its left side (3°), the way is again blocked by wet overhangs and a vertical undercut crack on the left must be taken for 15m (6°). A long traverse right (2°) leads into the chimney again then slabs are climbed on its right side for a rope length (3°) to a fourth impasse, in the form of a large chockstone. Bypass this by bridging between smooth wet walls (6°). The chimney above is then followed for 60m (4°, wet) and then a vast ramp of easy angled grey slabs are climbed for 120m (2°) out of the chimney and onto a large plateau on the crest of the pillar. About 6 hours from start. Shelter under boulders.

From the top right of the ledge, a narrow ramp leads up right for 60m (2°), eventually widening into a terrace which obligingly curves easily up the right side of the pillar and back to the next great ledge (1°). Another ramp goes right again from here onto a pedestal, and then a series of narrow grassy ledges interconnect up the right side of the pillar (1°, 2°, some moves 3°) until a large scree and snow ledge is reached beneath the summit towers. About 8 hours from start. (If necessary it may be possible to retreat from here down the long ramp to the left, to the foot of the Eastern Couloir.)

High above can be seen a ramp leading to the skyline on the right. Gain it by climbing up the left edge of a hanging snowfield for 120m (2°, 3°), then crossing the upper edge and ascending slabs rightwards for another 150m (2°, 3°) to the upper edge. A smaller ramp now goes right again out onto a steep tower (1°) then two pitches follow up the tower, first stepping left from the ramp, onto the undercut base and then trending left to a ledge (5°). Continue almost straight up the wall, by steep grooves (5°) to an easy angled ridge. Follow the ridge for 90m (1°) to a ledge of large broken blocks which is crossed to its right end. A further traverse of 15m right then a steep 30m wall (4°) lead to the scree slopes and the top.

143. DESCENT BY THE WEST RIDGE

Easy scrambling leads to the path down to the Stigfoss huts (Route 182). Alternatively, by descending scree and snow slopes to the north west, down past the snow basin and over the path from Trolltind, it is only ten minutes or so to the good bivouac under the large boulder in the moraine above Storgrovbotnen. Time to Stigfoss, 2 hours.

144. DESCENT BY THE SOUTH EAST RIDGE

Bypass the summit crags and descend the southern slopes (snow) before rejoining the lower part of the ridge which is followed until scree slopes can be descended between cliffs into Romsdal. 2–3 hours.

Søndre Trolltind (Semletind)
1,618m (5,307ft)

145. EAST PILLAR, ORIGINAL ROUTE
(A R Heen, P Svendsaas, L Eiknem. 1963)

There are no real technical difficulties but the route is extremely long and inescapable, with some objective dangers. It is therefore a fairly serious route for its low grade and the easiest way is not always obvious. The lower half up the great couloir between Søndre

Trolltind and Trollryggen may often be wet and is open to avalanches early in the season when there are many large hanging snowfields under the north wall. The traverse left and pillar are without difficulty but the upper wall which is above the north wall is extremely loose. The climb is nevertheless worthwhile in that it takes one through impressive rock scenery of an unusually forbidding nature. 5–8 hours. Over 2,000m of climbing. Grade III sup. Diags pgs 77, 81, 82 and 84.

Two approaches are possible, either by the path from Fiva (over 3km) or by crossing the river by the railway bridge from the main Romsdal road and walking back down the valley (about 1.5km from the road). Having reached the base of the huge slab couloir leading into the great gloomy rock bowl under the north wall, ascend first by grass to the left. Traverse right under a cliff and up the left edge of the couloir, until at the level of 'The Terrace' – the extremely long ledge under the north wall. This section is about 750m (some pitches 4°sup, or harder if care is not taken with choice of route).

Go easily along The Terrace (usually snow covered) and out onto the crest of the East Pillar, where it rises upwards to finish near the left edge, (possible bivouac sites under numerous boulders). From the top left end, ascend a short steep groove (4°) then trend rightwards up the pillar on easy angled rock to the second terrace (snow).

Above is the summit wall which is crossed low down by following an easy ramp rightwards until a steep crack and chimney is reached (4°). From here, move rightwards again until out above the North Wall, and ascend the easiest line of grooves and chimneys (5°, 3°, loose) finishing just right of the summit – often corniced early in the season.

146. HØIBAKK'S CHIMNEY
(A Hellewell, D Johnston. 1969)

The route lies up the impressive gash splitting the right (north) wall of the East Pillar from ground level to almost half height. The chimney was quite notorious, having defeated several European teams in the five years prior to its first ascent. The first and second attempts were made by Ralph Høibakk who discovered the route and pioneered all but the last five pitches. From the top of the chimney the route follows the East Pillar for 1,000m to the summit. The first complete ascent was made in three days, the chimney itself being 500m. Grade VI.

The base of the chimney is gained via a scree slope and a direct line up slabs. Begin by a steep rope length (5°) to a stance on the left arête, then 18m (6°) awkwardly round the overhanging chimney to a stance in the gully. Follow this for 60m (3°) then take the left wall to a V-corner and ascend by bridging to a nick, 45m (5°). Continue in the corner for 23m then leave delicately on the left wall (peg) to a belay in 8m (6°). Ascend by the left arête for a further 40m (4°) until the corner is regained. This leads in 18m to a cave. Bivouac.

Leave the cave on the left wall and climb via loose blocks for a rope length (3°) to a stance. Continue for 25m up the gully (6°) to a steep chimney (usually wet) with two chockstones high up, which is climbed in 33m (4°) to a small cave; good stance. Now on small holds leave the cave directly and traverse left to a steep grass ledge with a shrub for aid, and so to a nick, 45m (6°). Traverse right from here and up to a ledge with high flakes, 25m (5°), good stance. From the uppermost flake reach a bolt (in situ) and make an awkward reach left to a crack. Peg this for 25m to a large grass ledge, 45m (A3). Bivouac.

From here continue for two rope lengths (4°) up the chimney to a cave, then a third rope length (5°) out

right under overhangs and across slabs, moving up to a protruding block (stance) below an overhanging crack. Peg the crack, then still using pegs for aid, move out left and step over the top of the chimney onto the slabs of the East Pillar.

Follow the East Pillar route for 1,000m (3°,4°) to the summit.

147. NORTH FACE, LEFT-HAND DIHEDRALS
(A C Wilmott, S Eskell 1969. First free ascent Jun 1978, F Martinsen, H Doseth)

A very fine route and a fitting memorial to Tony Wilmott, a great character and one of Britain's best young climbers of his day, sadly killed in the Avon Gorge in 1970. The route takes a good natural line, almost totally independent. The difficulties are mainly sustained free climbing in the upper half which takes the obvious series of corners running up the upper north face about 250m left of the Direct Route. The climb starts at the same

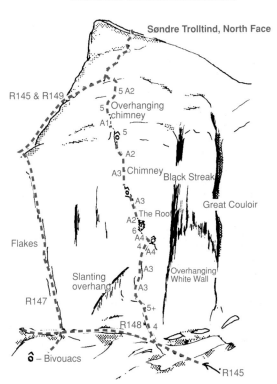

Søndre Trolltind, North Face

R145 & R149

5 A2

5 Overhanging chimney

A1

5

A2

A3 Chimney

Black Streak

Great Couloir

A3

The Roof

A2

6

A4

Flakes

4 A4

A3

Overhanging White Wall

Slanting overhang

A3

R147

5+

R148 4

δ̂ – Bivouacs

R145

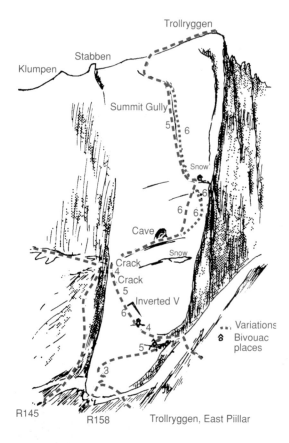

Trollryggen, East Piillar

pitch, (45m, 5°). Straight up above, to a chimney and up this to a good stance (37m, 4°). Continue up right for two rope lengths (3°) then straight up for 18m (2°) to ledges below and slightly left of an overhanging V-chimney. The object of the game is to reach a grass patch just right of the half-way point in the chimney. Climb straight up above the stance to flakes at 7m. Place a peg then go up right across the wall (2 pegs) and across a large detached flake to reach a sapling in the chimney. Escape rightwards using a peg, to gain the tiny grass patch with difficulty. Layback the wall above to good spike belays (25m, 6°sup, A1).

Layback the crack up right to easier ground. Go up left and belay after 45m (6°). Continue up left for two rope lengths (3°) to the great terrace cutting across below the upper North Face.

Move right along this for over 100m, passing below an obvious series of caverns on the face above, to an obvious line of weakness leading up left to a big black cave. Follow this for 60m to a steep corner (3°) then move steeply out left and up to the cave (45m, 4°). Up the steep crack just left of the huge spike (45m, 6°, sling to start). Continue up the same line to a cave at the foot of a huge corner (45m, 5°, 45m, 4°).

Layback and bridge out round the chockstone roof then up a groove to a second cave. Up the rib and wall on the right to a small stance (42m, 6°). Move left into the corner and up to a roof. Layback this to the left, peg, then up the groove above using six pegs and slings to exit free with difficulty to a stance in a chimney (37m, 6°sup, A1). Move up right then back left across the roof using a sling on the lip. Continue in the same

point as Høibakk's Chimney, at the top of the scree cone which is about 1 hour from the road, crossing the river by the railway bridge. The first ascent took two days, with a bivouac just below the terrace and one on the summit: climbing time about 26 hrs. 1,650m. Grade VI sup. Diag pg 81.

Climb slabs by zig-zags, somewhat to the right of the chimney runnel (4°, 3°). Continue straight up for well over 100m (2°) to an amphitheatre hemmed in by steeper rock. Follow a line of corners up and to the right for 90m (3°) to more slabs. Up these for about 180m (2°) via some scree ledges going to the right after 90m and then up some broken corners in the upper half to a second gully/amphitheatre, which has a steep black wall on the left. Climb a ramp going out left across this wall with a split crack at 30m until below an obvious line of weakness – a magnificent line to a huge perched block (45m, 5°). Climb the slab up left (12m, 4°) then go straight up to meet easier ground (42m, 5°). Up left via a short chimney to gain another corner, (42m, 4°). Go straight up the corner for 45m (5°) to a good ledge.

From here, a series of good ledges are followed leftwards onto the upper section of the East Pillar, which is followed for 240m to the summit (3°, 4°).

148. NORTH WALL
(R Baillie, J Amatt. 1967)

A very steep route with fine situations; exposed but safe with straightforward route finding. The difficulties are mainly sustained and hard artificial climbing on the vertical wall. The latest American techniques and equipment were used on the first ascent, making it relatively fast. No pegs were left in place and consequently skyhooks, rurps, and a complete range of American pegs are necessary, including bongs up to 4" (100mm). The introductory and final sections are as for the East Pillar, Original. On the wall itself ledges are very small and bivouac hammocks are an asset. No water is available on this section. 4 days. 1,650m. Grade VI sup.

Ascend the Slab Couloir (Route 145) into the rock bowl under the wall (750m, some pitches 4°sup, or harder if care is not taken with choice of route). From the highest point of the snow climb a 30m wall to gain the traverse line leading left to prominent broken chimneys, which are followed to their top (90m, 4°, 5°sup). Continue by the obvious series of shallow grooves to the right of the big overhangs (54m, A3) to a stance in etriers below the overhanging chimney. Climb the chimney which is very awkward (18m, A4, sky hooks, 4" (100mm) bongs and wide angles) to flakes which lead to a small ledge (4°). First bivouac.

Traverse left for 9m and enter the deep groove below the large triangular overhang 'The Roof' (36m, 6°, A4, skyhooks). From a belay in etriers, turn The Roof on the left (8m, A2) and climb the groove through the

overhangs above to a small ledge on the left (60m, A2, A3, 5°, belay in etriers midway). Second bivouac.

Good cracks above (A2) lead to a wide crack on the right wall of the chimney (30m, A3). Follow the groove above (good bivouac ledge at 30m) to a small ledge (60m, A2). Turn the overhang on the left and climb a short corner (33m, 5°, A2) before traversing left and up to ledges at the base of 'The Finger of Fate' (36m, 5°, A2). Third bivouac behind the flake. (NB 1979. The 'Fickle Finger of Fate' collapsed, a new pitch of 5°, A2, rejoins the original).

Climb the chimney to the top of the flake and the short crack above to a ledge on the left (36m, 5°). Continue up cracks for a

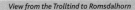
View from the Trolltind to Romsdalshorn

further 36m (A2) to a belay in etriers below the overhanging chimney. Ascend the chimney for 30m through overhangs (5°) to a big ledge, and then up the overhanging chimney on the right (36m, 5°, A2). Traverse left to easy ground and ascend to the summit by moving right to avoid difficulties, finishing up the final wall of the East Pillar Route, 300m (5°,4°, 3°, loose).

The next route is out on the front of the great pillar which rises from the valley up the left edge of the North Face.

149. THE EAST PILLAR
(A Howard, B Tweedale, R Holt, W Gartside. 1967)

This is the central of Romsdal's famous 'Three Pillars' it gives a very long and therefore quite serious route but the standard is nowhere excessive and the first pitch is as hard as any. The route follows a long groove on the left side of the pillar, then ascends bald bulging slabs on the nose by comparatively easy grooves (complex route finding) until The Terrace of the Original Route (Route 145) is reached. The Original Route is then followed to the summit with care on the loose headwall. A recommendable route and a good introduction to its harder neighbours. 9–11 hours. Over 2,000m. Grade IV sup. Photo pg 79.

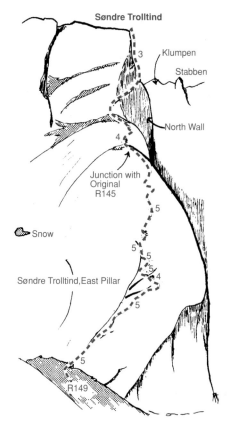

The start of the climb is in the obvious long groove slanting up into the pillar from the snow patch at the mouth of the enormous couloir between Søndre Trolltind and Breitind. It is best approached by crossing the river by the railway bridge from the main Romsdal road and then up through trees and snowfields. This is a little over 1km whereas from Fiva Farm it is over 3km.

The foot of the obvious slanting groove is about 45m right of the couloir mouth. After crossing the bergschrund it may be followed exactly, or approached by slabs on its right; either way is 45m (5°). Continue in the same line as the groove up polished glaciated slabs for about four rope lengths (3°, 2°) till the rock steepens again. A pitch up a groove (3°) leads to a ledge some

distance beneath two obvious black overlaps. Avoid them by ascending diagonally right (awkward, 5°) to a large grass ledge leading rightwards onto the crest of the pillar.

From the right end of the ledge, zig-zag easily up left into a chimney. Climb this (4°) then go left again to regain the original groove above the black overlaps. Up this (5°, wet), then a second, smaller detour right then up and back left by a hidden groove and an exposed traverse into the main groove again. Two steep pitches up cracks and corners (5°) lead to a ledge. Take the open groove from its right end (3°) then up ledges and a steep chimney (5°). Zig-zagging up further ledges on the broad nose of the pillar lead to The Terrace, snow; junction with the Original Route which is then followed to the summit, (some 5°, loose).

150. DESCENT BY THE SOUTH WEST SIDE

An easy scramble on scree and snow to join the Stigfoss path (Route 182) near the boulder bivouac on the rim of Storgrovbotn. ('/₄ hour). 2–3 hours to the road at the top of Stigfoss.

151. THE SØNDRE TROLLTIND–BREITIND (AND STIGHORN) RIDGE

A pleasant walk with good views of the Trolltinder and an awe-inspiring view down the 600m overhanging wall into the rock bowl under Søndre Trolltind (Semletind). Much snow in the early season. 7 hours, Grade II inf.

Follow Route 182, until below the col between the south ridge of Trollryggen and the north west side of Søndre Trolltind. Scramble up scree and snow to the col which is a square cut edge above the 600m wall, and then continue up scree slopes to the top of Søndre Trolltind – often corniced above the north wall in the early season.

Descend to the south, this time on the rim of the great corrie north of Breitind, which is again often corniced, and up scree and snow to the summit of Breitind (a good viewpoint).

Descend from Breitind by the South East Ridge (Route 144) and into Romsdal, or preferably return down Alnesdalen, a distance of 7km to the top of Stigfoss. One can of course, also descend by the South West Ridge of Breitind and then, by subsidiary peaks with a little climbing, ascend to the top of Stighorn. The south side of Stighorn is then descended to Alnesvatn and Stigfoss (Route 218).

Next, three routes on small pinnacles poised above Romsdal:

Klumpen

152. SOUTH EAST RIDGE
(Party unknown)

This is the first rounded pinnacle on the South East Ridge of Trollryggen. It gives a

pleasant little climb up the ridge. 60m. Grade II. Diag pg 82.

From the col, climb easy angled slabs keeping as close to the edge (and the 600m drop) as one desires, then left a little and up a fairly steep crack (2°) to the top. Descend easily to the north.

Stabben

153. WEST FACE
(E Birkeland, O Nygard. 1926)

An easy little climb on good, rough rock. 60m. Grade II. Diag pg 82.

Climb by almost any line (2°), the normal start being low on the right.

154. NORTH CHIMNEY
(A R Heen and party)

Nice climbing on a short but impressively steep wall. The route starts at the obvious narrow chimney about 15m below its north col. 45m. Grade II sup.

Follow the chimney-crack, first up steeply (3°), then bearing right onto the western slabs which are climbed to the summit.

Trollryggen 1,742m (5,723ft)

155. SOUTH WEST SIDE: ORDINARY ROUTE
(Fieve, J Venge. 1880)

An easy route, rarely used except in descent. 3 hours. Grade I.

Follow the path up from Stigfoss (Route 182) until beneath Klumpen. Leave the main cairned path and ascend by scree and snow, passing close beneath Stabben. Continue up scree on the southern slopes with some scrambling to the top.

156. SOUTH EAST RIDGE
(Party unknown)

An interesting ridge scramble if no diversions are made. 3 hours. Grade II.

Follow Route 151 to the col above the 600m Romsdal Wall and then up to the top of Klumpen by the South East Ridge (II). Descend easily northwards and along to Stabben which is climbed by its West Face (II). Descend from Stabben by an abseil down its vertical north wall and then scramble easily along the south east ridge, keeping close to the edge, to the summit of Trollryggen.

Approaching directly from Romsdal itself, is:

157. SOUTH EAST WALL – MIDDLE ROUTE
(Michael Orolin, Jaromir Soldan, Daniel Bakos, Vladimir Petrik. 25 Feb–7 Mar 1974)

The route was first climbed in winter, using 200 pitons (70 were left in place) also 20 wooden wedges and 9 expansion bolts (7 were for stances). The lower part of the wall was climbed in water-ice for 250m. Fixed ropes were used to the first bivouac, the first three days of climbing were from bivouacs in the camp under the wall. The following description reflects the winter conditions at the time of the first ascent which took nine days. 1,600m of climbing, height of the wall 1,200m. Grade VI sup.

Follow Route 145 to the basin under the East Wall, then start at the lowest point of the pillar in the couloir. Flake diedres lead from left to right (5°, A1). An overhang (6°, A1) and a little obvious diedre lead to a steep and overhanging chimney to small platforms (5°sup, first bivouac) 250m from start. From the platforms traverse left to a 15m steep diedre 35m (A2, A4) and left to the platform. Second bivouac.

Traverse 20m left to steep flake wall. Up by a crack to the stance with expansion bolts (A2). Little left using knife blades (A3) and then directly to the terrace (6°, A2). Third bivouac.

From the left end, ascend to the diedre, 40m (5°, A2). The diedre follows to a narrow chimney. Up this, with wooden wedges over the overhang. Traverse left using expansion bolt to new diedre, (A2, A4, 6°). 5m up, then a little left to its end beneath an overhang.

10m traverse left (4°). Easier for 150m, sloping right to the terrace under the Grey Tower (3°, 4°). Fourth bivouac.

From the big 'schrund beneath the top of Grey Tower for 200m (one place 4°) to below the summit wall. From the col behind the tower a diedre goes to the right, 30m on blocks (4°sup). Traverse to the left 10m under overhanging diedre, which is climbed for 7m (4°). Left to the slab, and directly up onto the overhang and move right (5°) to diedre, follow this to the summit icefield (6°). 250–300m steep snowfield to the top.

The big pillar on the right is the third of Romsdal's Three Pillars. It was the scene of the first of Romsdal's long, serious routes and, like the other two, is amongst Europe's longest rock climbs:

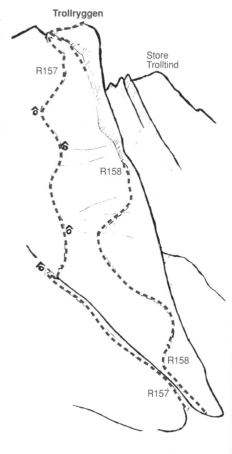

158. EAST PILLAR
(R Høibakk, A R Heen. 1958)

The most difficult of Romsdal's 'Three Pillars' – its first ascent was a breakthrough in Norway's mountaineering history. It was the sixth attempt, no previous party having reached much beyond The Cave. The greatest problem is route finding through complex slab systems which make the route very long and serious. The section between The Cave and the Summit Gully is particularly complicated and the route described here is not necessarily that of the first ascent. There are a number of 6° pitches and, if the correct route is not located, some artificial climbing may be necessary. Further, a descent from high on the pillar is difficult. It is therefore essential to carry a dozen pegs or more as precautions against these eventualities. Bivouac places are more than adequate and often palatial. There is almost always enough snow for water. First ascent about 16 hours (12 hours from the first Bivouac). Most following successful ascents have required at least two full days though the fastest time is 14 hours with no bivouac. Recommended bivouac sites are The Cave, the foot of the Summit Gully or an excellent ledge two-thirds way between them, below a chimney. Over 2,000m. Grade VI inf. Photos and diags pgs 77, 79, 82, 86, 87.

The snow patch at the bottom of the East Pillar is reached in about 1 hour from Fiva Farm. Gain the slabs from the left (3°) or by traversing in from the right-hand side of the snow slopes (4°sup). Solo easily up the first band of steep rock which is taken most easily on the right (3°) and keep right for a total distance of about five rope lengths (some moves 4°) until steep rock is reached again. With careful route finding a way is found through the barrier (60m, 4°sup) by a chimney towards the left. Alternatively, this point can be reached in two hours from Fiva Farm by ascending the screes until level with it, then via a groove (3°) above the bergschrund to a long leftward traverse (90m, 4°sup) leading to the grassy terrace below the barrier.

From terraces above the barrier (bivouac, first ascent) trend easily up left towards the

conspicuous inverted V. Continue left beneath it by a delicate slab (5°sup) and an easy crack leading to a 9m vertical chimney in the left wall of the V. Ascend this (6°, peg) and follow the long ramp rising across the south side of the Pillar (mostly 2° and 3° with two pitches 4°) until it ends at a corner above some blocks. After the corner (3°) go easily right on plateau (snow), through some slabs (3°), and right again easily to The Cave (bivouac).

Continue right from here along the highest narrow ledge until it ends at an open groove. Move diagonally right into this on stepped rock and ascend it (5°) to a stance on the left. Continue up the steep groove (6°, pegs) before traversing right on ledges and ascending a short wall (5°). A hidden crack is now climbed on the left (4°sup) until more ledges enable a rightward traverse to be made to within 9m of the edge where a short corner leads to a platform. Climb the thin crack on its right (6° pegs) over a bulging slab and

R158

continue up a long groove, still with difficulty, until it ends on an excellent grass ledge beneath an overhang (bivouac).

Continue in the same line by a chimney (4°sup) to terraces and then by loose grooves and chimneys (4°) for four pitches to the foot of the Summit Gully (bivouac, snow). (The Norwegian Troll Wall Route joins here). Climb the gully for two rope lengths (3°) and then either move out onto its left ridge or continue up the gully. In wet conditions the former may be preferable and is climbed as on the first ascent until a steep wall is reached at midway (4°, 5°, loose rock). Avoid the wall by traversing delicately right across the side wall (5°sup) and then move up onto the ridge again. Easier climbing above leads onto the scree and snow ledges above the gully.

If the gully is chosen it is followed until a corner is seen high on the left wall. Gain it by ascending the chimney and traversing across steep rock (5°), then ascend the corner directly on good rock (6°, pegs). Alternatively, the chimney, if dry, may be followed throughout (6°). Continue up the gully above, passing the next barrier by a narrow chimney on the left (4°sup). Higher up, the gully splits again and a chimney-groove on the right is taken (5°), escaping through a hole after which a pitch of easy slabs trending left leads to the aforementioned scree and snow ledges. Go easily left across these by the scar on the south east ridge (bivouac site to left, through the gap) and follow the ridge easily to the top.

The Troll Wall

Otherwise known as Trollveggen, this is Norway's biggest and most famous rock wall ranking equal to anything in Europe. It remained unclimbed until 1965 when the news that a British team was going to attempt 'The Wall' was passed on by Arne Randers Heen to a group of Norwegian climbers. They consequently tried to pre-empt the British by getting a rope on the wall first, laying claim to a line which unfortunately was a false start. The Brits began the next day up a line they had chosen on a recce the previous winter, now known as The Rimmon Route (named after their Climbing Club). Whilst the press made a big story of the two 'competitive' climbs, all the climbers got on very well together and the Grand Hotel in Åndalsnes

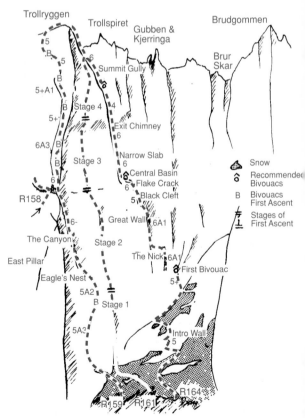

Trollryggen North Face - Trollveggen or Troll Wall

together with the tourism office hosted a big party for all concerned when the two teams completed their climbs.

Since then, numerous routes have been climbed on the wall and the Rimmon Route which was eventually climbed free became a classic, later described by John Middendorf and Aslak Aastorp as 'a masterpiece of route finding at the highest free and aid standards of the day'. The other big free classic on The Wall was the Swedish Route. Sadly, both The Rimmon and Swedish Routes were destroyed by a huge rockfall in 1998. Details are retained here for historical interest along with those of other pioneering routes on The Wall. Further details and topos are in the *Klatring i Romsdal* guide. The latest new routes to be added to the Troll Wall are two Russian Routes climbed in 1997 before the rockfall.

The summit of The Wall is called Trollryggen, but many famous pinnacles line its top: these are the Trolls - beware they don't get angry!

Warning As in the Alps and other high mountains, global warming seems to be taking its toll: since September 1998 there have been some massive rockfalls on the wall possibly due to ice trapped within the mountain since the last ice age melting, forcing off and releasing the surface of the wall. Much of the Rimmon (English) and Swedish Routes has been destroyed along with other nearby routes. Rockfalls are still continuing. Local climbers say it's chaos up there. Much of the right side of the wall is considered insecure and advice should be sought from local climbers before attempting any route on the face.

June/July is probably the best time for climbing any of Romsdal's north facing walls because it is daylight almost round the clock. There are even a couple of hours of direct sunlight on the Troll Wall in early morning. Also, there may be snow for water on the bigger ledges in early summer. However, during the snow melt period (about midsummer) before the Upper Snowfield below the back of the wall has stabilised, the approach up the scree slope and Intro Wall can be subject to dangerous avalanches. (This part of the wall may be taboo anyway since the rockfalls.) Temperatures can be the same day or night so beware of avalanches at any time. The following route, which is close to the left edge, seems unaffected:

TROLL WALL
Lower half of
Norwegian Route

159. THE NORWEGIAN ROUTE

(*L Pettersen, J Teigland, O D Enersen, O Eliassen. 1965*)

A long and difficult route of sustained severity, attacking Trollveggen (the Troll Wall) by its left side and escaping at half height by a huge corner – The Canyon – onto the snowfield at the base of the Summit Gully on the East Pillar. From then on, the route takes a line up the prominent groove on the left arête of The Wall to the summit. The party who started the climb at the same time as the British in 1965 were on The Wall for 11 days on the first ascent (eight days climbing). Bivouac sites are usually good and there is normally sufficient water until the latter half of the season. Both halves of the route are very exposed but an escape is possible by the East Pillar climb at halfway. Few pitons were left in place and the route had not been repeated in 1979 though it was climbed free in 1986. A large number and variety of pegs was used on the first ascent. The rock is mostly good on the Lower Wall, but deteriorates on the upper half. 1,500m. Grade VI sup. Photos and diags pgs 88, 89 and 91.

The lower half of the Norwegian Route received a second ascent by Eric Lackner, Michael von Gizycki and James Skone in 20 hours' non-stop climbing after a preliminary preparation of the first three pitches. Because of doubtful weather the ascent was completed by the ordinary East Pillar Route on the second day. Skone describes the route as 'more dangerous than difficult, with mostly free climbing on loose vegetated rock, especially between the central terraces. On this occasion no water could be found on the route until a snow patch at the bottom of The Canyon, about 80m below the East Pillar. The original guidebook description and gradings (as below) are not very accurate; see topo for improved details. About 15 pegs were found, mainly on stances; 30 more should be taken. The fixed rope left on the 6°inf groove of pitch 4 from the first ascent is in a dangerous state. This pitch could probably be split at the beginning of the groove.'

The last eight pitches (190m) of the route were also climbed during the first ascent of the Arch Wall (Route 160). See that route for a comparative description.

The route begins up a snow finger projecting up left from scree and snow slopes into the lower left part of Trollveggen. Approach from Fiva Farm (1½–3 hrs) and ascend the snow ramp to its highest right-hand point. Cross the bergschrund and ascend directly for 30m (4°) before traversing left across broad vertical ribs (4° sup) for a rope length. Continue up left before reaching loose rocks in a gully, which is followed to a good belay (39m, 5°, A3). Follow the gully for another rope length (4°, 5°sup) working left, then up and back right to a platform. From the left end of the platform ascend a slab which ends in a crack (5° A2). Belay in etriers. Follow the crack until it disappears, then move left and up (5°sup A1). Belay on poor pegs. Good bivouac 24m right.

From the belay, trend right for 39m (3°, 4°) and continue right up loose rock for another rope length (4°). Trend right again for 39m (4°, 5°, A2), moving up to ledges. Follow these right and left easily for almost 90m (1°) to a perfect bivouac site – The Eagle's Nest.

From the bivouac, climb for two rope lengths (4°sup) first bearing left on large rocks, then straight up and to the right in a little gully. This is followed for another two rope lengths, passing overhanging rocks on their left (4°) to a small hole. Move out of the hole and round two corners for 39m (4°sup) to The Canyon (snow). This is the big diedre visible from below. Follow cracks up the 70m Wall on its left side (6°inf), to the snow patch on the East Pillar of Trollryggen. Bivouac and junction with the East Pillar Route.

From the bivouac ascend the ridge on the right (5°) for 30m to a belay at the top of The Canyon, then easily (1°) for two pitches to a belay 9m left of the edge of Trollveggen. Move out onto the wall and up for 3m to a belay (6°) before stepping right and up a gully to overhangs. Avoid them by moving into another gully which is still overhanging but leads to a good belay under a ceiling (27m 6°). Traverse below the roof until it is possible to move up to its top (5°) and into another gully. Follow this (5°, 3°sup) to its end where there is a possible bivouac site though a better one will be found 9m higher.

1965 attempt

R161 R164

R159

Climb the gully for two pitches (4°sup, 5°) to its end, then move left and down for 39m (3°, 4°, very loose). Continue left for 21m then up to a large platform (4°). Bear right then follow the platform left for a rope length (3°) continuing left then up an overhanging crack (5°sup) for a pitch. Now, on extremely loose rock, go up and left to more ledges (4°) then left again to a smaller platform at 30m. Go over slabs to the right towards a crack, and up this to an overhanging crack (5°) which is climbed on its right; a further 15m moving left over slabs (5°) and then a final crack leads to the ridge just below the summit.

160. ARCH WALL
(H and E Ward Drummond. Aug 1972)

This climb is a serious multi-day route which the origina-tors classed on the Yosemite method as Grade 6, 5.9, A5. Owing to food shortage and serious frostbite the first ascent team finished up the last few pitches of the Norwegian Route. (An optional finish is now provided by the route of Baltika climbed up the left edge of the wall in 1997 by Odintsov and Potankin – see Klatring i Romsdal.*) The first ascent took 21 days of which seven were lost owing to bad weather. 1,200m. Grade VI sup.*

In their account of the first ascent the Drummonds made the following useful logistical notes:

'Although the route could be climbed in ten days this would only be possible in perfect weather. As this is unlikely additional food should be taken: dehydrated food is particu-larly good from the point of view of core warmth. Some kind of easily erected tent is

Traverse out right for 21m and up a crack for 9m (4°). Leave this on the right and move back out onto Trollveggen for a rope length (6°) to a poor belay. 30m of extremely difficult artificial climbing above (6°, A3, loose) leads to platforms. Good bivouac site with water.

Follow the crack, bearing right for a rope length (3°) then straight up, left, back towards the crack (5°). Follow the crack again for 21m to a small rock ceiling (5°sup), passing it on its right and continuing for a rope length (4°sup) to a niche. Straight up for 9m (3°) to a bivouac.

Ascend the right side of a gully (5°) for a rope length then go left for a second rope length into a small groove (5° A1), moving left at the bottom of a gully where there is a poor bivouac site.

essential. On this ascent a home-made 8oz nylon tube tent, press-studded along its sides, was used. Karrimats or other non-absorbing insulators were invaluable in preventing exposure during long wet sit-ins. Polar suits over two layers of Damart underwear were worn for bivouacking and climbing, since down would rapidly have become sodden. Hammocks were necessary at several of the bivouac sites'.

'A total of about 90kg of gear, food, and water (1.5 litres per person per day) was hauled in three bags as far as the Great Flake, then two bags were adequate. Water can be collected at a drip just above the main Great Flake ledge system'.

'New ropes for climbing and hauling are recommended to minimise danger from wear. 50m ropes were used. Pegs carried comprised nine bongs (2"–3"), 26 angles ($\frac{1}{2}$"–1$\frac{1}{2}$"), four thin Leepers, 18 assorted Lost Arrows, nine thin blades (Hitens and Bugaboos), and five each Crack Tacks and Rurps. 15 wedges on wire from Moac to smallest Cracker, were also taken. The short thin knife blades were particularly useful and at least ten should be carried to allow for damage: the Chouinard ones were too soft and the short thin Hitens cracked at the junction of head and blade. Skyhooks are essential, but all necessary bolts are in place at belays and on the pitches (two aid, one protection). Just over half the route is artificial; all the hard pitches and many of the others have both free and aid climbing, requiring a smooth change from one to the other'.

The following description uses English grades:
1/2: 68m. 5a. Climb the introductory slabs to the left end of the huge overhang at the bottom right corner of the huge smooth wall between the French and Rimmon routes. Get the haul bags up here out of the weather before tackling the next two pitches, which are particularly difficult for hauling and climbing respectively.
3: 37m. 5b. A short easy left traverse from bolt belay beneath overhanging ribs gives access to big slab leading to short flared chimney with bolt belay at its top.
4: 37m. A5.5a. The crack above, free, then

under the roof to its right end. Then vague cracks up the wall, some free, to poor ledges (hammock bivouac).
5: 43m, A2, 5b. The perfect pitch: a few pegs to start, then free to a hanging bolt stance.
6: 40m, A2, 4c. The groove above, mixed, to Lindy's ledge: bivouac two.
7: 46m, A4, 5b. Straight up the groove above (2 bolts for aid, skyhooks and free) to a smooth V-groove. Up this (A1) to a good ledge above the roof.
8: 21 m, 4b. Left on loose rock, free and up to good ledge.
9: 31 m, A3, 5a. Left to end of ledge then a few pegs, cross slab to left then steep free to good ledges.
10: 34m, A3, 4c. 6m left then up steep grooves with right traverse at 12m then steeply up to rubbly ledges. Bivouac three on Lucky's ledge down to left.
11: 31m, 5a. 5m right then up awkward free trending slightly right for 20m to good ledge.
12: 12m, A1, 4c. Left into short smooth groove and up to good ledge on right.
13: 34m, A4, 5a. Move left onto steep wall, up and left with two bad pegs to rough groove round corner. Up for 15m hard free to hanging belay on tiny ledges where groove steepens.
14: 46m, A2, 5a. Follow the crack trending left in a superb position to ledges at end. Then 12m free straight up until one can move left into good crack in smooth groove just below ledges (House of Heen, bivouac four).
15: 46m, A2, 5b. First ferry the haul bags down to lowest ledges on left. Trend left up wall, climbing the difficult V groove with one peg to begin. Trend left to big platform with belays at back.
16: 18m, 4b. Up loose blocks to left then across broken ledges to good bivouac at far left, more or less out of the drips (Great Flake ledges, bivouac five).

(The line now crosses the French route. After the Big Swing (pitch 20) escape is virtually impossible, so leave the haul line as a back rope to the Great Flake ledges until the pendulum has been done successfully.)
17: 46m, A2, 5a. As for the French route: easily back and up to right onto big platform (split the pitch here). Free then mixed up the

groove behind the platform to good ledge.
18: 31m, A2, 5a. Move left up groove, mixed, then trend left up steep wall (free) and loose blocks to good ledge.
19: 12m, 5b. Hand traverse left and up with difficulty to good ledge.
20: 37m, A4. Descend rope for about 30m and pendulum across to foot of groove on left. Difficult aid in last few feet.
21: 15m, A2. Up groove past detached blocks then step left onto small platform.
22: 31 m, A5, 5b. Free climb the black groove ahead using a couple of skyhooks and two pegs for aid, to hanging bolt belay.
23: 31m, A4, 5a. Thin pegging slightly right until possible to free climb across to small but good ledge on left, about 15m below the huge roof of the Arch.
24: 37m, A3, 4c. Hard free to left, then straight up with awkward aid to good crack at left end of the Arch. Follow the crack until just below left end of roof, then free climb across small ledges to right end of Arch (bivouac six).
25: A2. A magnificent pitch: follow the roofs out right until the vertical crack splitting the wall above can be gained. Belay about 6m up.
26: 25m, 5b. Free climb the shallow crack with difficulty, then the crack on left with a point or two of aid to good small ledge (the Altar, bivouac seven).
27: 34m, 5a. Diagonally left with difficulty to enter a short groove leading to slab beneath overhanging black groove.
28: 43m, A3, 5a. Up the groove, partly free, moving left at top beneath roofs to thin crack round corner. Up this to belay on smooth slabs where angle eases.
29: 31m, 5a. Up behind belay to protection bolt then left into thin crack. Up this and groove above to good ledge.
30: 31 m, 4c. Move right across easy angled slab then up short steep corner.
31: 25m, 5a. Traverse left into crack, up it, and left across slab to good ledge below short corner.

The remaining eight pitches are as for the Norwegian Route.
32: 18m, 4c. Up corner to belay at fault on loose blocks.
33: 31 m, 4c. Traverse 12m left then climb

chimney over huge loose blocks. At top move right on good flakes to belay on top of huge flake.
34: 15m, 4b. Up groove above to easier ground and belay on left.
35/37: 46m, 4c. Traverse left until below broken groove.
38: 18m, 4b. Up groove to ledges and belay in good crack to right.
39: 28m, 4c. Up behind belay then crack above. Traverse awkwardly right then climb steep wall, moving left at top to belay below broken corner.
40: 18m, 5a. Up behind belay then over big loose blocks into groove capped by enormous chockstone. Free past left side of this to belay on slab above.
41: 15m, 5a. Easily left then up short overhanging wall to the summit.

161. THE FRENCH DIRECT ROUTE
(Deck, Boussard, Cordier, Brunet, Frehel. 1967)

A magnificent and tremendously serious route taking a direct line up the Troll Wall, starting up hidden diedres right of the Norwegian Route, and directly beneath the summit of Trollryggen. The route is predominately artificial with pitches up to A4, requiring 40 pegs, and very little free climbing beneath 5°inf. It may be described in four parts, beginning with the Lower Wall which has one very difficult pitch (3 bolts). Next is the Second Wall, mostly artificial and vertical – the last pitch is free. Above is the great black and white Third Wall, some free to begin with but again mostly artificial, often on loose rock and finishing up the Big Overhangs – one of 2.5m, others of 1m. Finally, the Summit Wall described by the first party as 'not so easy and long enough'.

The first ascent (from which this description is taken) took 21 days – 14 climbing days. They used over 600 pegs, mostly American of all sizes, many wooden wedges and 'a lot of other sorts'. 800m of rope was fixed to a point above the Big Overhangs. About 80 pegs were left in place, some dangerous, and one rappel rope, dangerous. Water is a problem, none being available once the Lower Wall has been passed. No stone fall

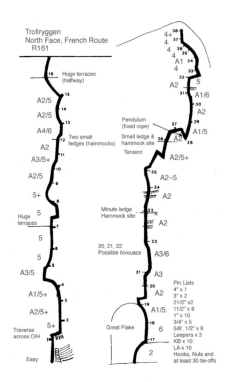

Trollryggen
North Face, French Route
R161

attempt was aborted some 3½ pitches above the Great Flake on the fourth day as water supplies were too low to justify continuing after a false line had been taken. It was found possible to escape onto the East shoulder at the level of the Great Flake (see Route 162).

In contrast with the French, the British party encountered rockfall. They had one haul rope severed and a climbing rope badly damaged by loose rocks dislodged by haul bags etc. Much loose rock was reported on ledges and some even on overhanging pitches. At one point, the end of the second pitch above the Great Flake, loose rock constitutes a real danger.

No sign was found of the French bolts and thus it would appear that the British party climbed a variation at some point, probably the fourth pitch. The lower half of the face up to the Great Flake was found to comprise 15 pitches. About half the lower walls were found to be free – from 'loose 6° to occasional 6°sup'. Aid varies from A1 to A4. A start from a bivouac at the foot of the face should guarantee a reasonably fast party reaching half height in two days.

The discovery of the traverse to the east shoulder has undoubtedly detracted from the seriousness of this part of the face, particularly since the traverse would be possible in either direction. It is not, however, likely to detract from the seriousness of the upper half of the wall. Using the techniques adopted in this second attempt, the French Route should be possible in six days. 1,200m. Grade VI sup.

Pin list from first ascent: Angles, 1 @ 4", 2 @ 3", 2 @ 2½", 8 @ 1½", 10 @ 1", 5 @ ¾", 8 @ ⅝"–½", 3 Leepers, 10 King Pins, 10 Lost Arrows, hooks, nuts and at least 30 tie-offs.

FRENCH DESCRIPTION – LOWER WALLS.

Stage 1. Start the climb from snow slopes right of the Norwegian Route and ascend a groove in slabby rock (2°, 5°inf), slightly leftwards, then back right below the steep Lower Wall to a good belay ledge with blocks. Continue by a steep pitch (5°, A1)

was noted. Further parties should carry 100 to 150 pegs including 20 to 30 bongs or wedges. Jumars and a light winch are also recommended. It is possible a future ascent could be made by three climbers well versed in American techniques in about ten days. 1,200m. Grade VI sup. Photo pg 91.

SECOND ATTEMPT
(D Pearce and E Ward Drummond. Jul 1969)

Since the previous notes were written details became available of the British attempt on the route. This was to be the first continuous attempt, ie eschewing siege tactics. Though the attempt was finally abandoned through lack of water, there are considerable differences between the experiences and route descriptions of the French and British groups. Both are given below:

In the British attempt food and water were carried for six days as it was hoped to reach the Great Flake in two days, and the Upper Walls were expected to take four days. The

View past the Troll Wall to Romsdal from Nordre Trolltind

with some dulfer moves and a short over-hanging wall. Then make a difficult leftwards traverse (3 bolts) to a diedre. Ascend this and blocks above (A3, A4) to another diedre. Trend left up this (5°, A1) then traverse easily up left on ledges and slightly back right (some moves 4°sup) to a good bivouac site. This is just higher (and right) of the Eagle's Nest on the Norwegian Route, and below the vertical Second Wall. About one day.

Stage 2. Climb almost directly for three or four rope lengths of hard artificial (A1, A2, A3), then trend slightly right over overhangs (A3 many pegs) to the diedre. (Here is the rappel rope; do not use, dangerous.) Climb the diedre (A1, A2, 5°sup, very wet) until ledges are reached leading to the ledge and bivouac site (wet), beneath the Third Wall; about four days.

ENGLISH DESCRIPTION – LOWER WALLS

Start at the foot of a groove leading up to twin grooves capped by overhangs some 120m further up the screes from the Norwegian Route. From a point 60m up the easy groove it is possible to traverse right into the main groove system. Up this for three pitches (free, A2, A3) until it is possible to break out leftwards after 9m of A3 on fourth pitch, into an area of steep vegetation and loose rock. Up the terraces for several pitches to the foot of a clean cut groove somewhat on the left. Suggested bivi number one (three pitches from foot of wall).

Up the dihedral (A2) and slightly rightwards to a wet ledge (A3 and 6°sup). Continue up the crack above (A3) to ledges. Move right using a skyhook round the arête and up the wall above (A4 and 6°sup), to a stance. Up the wide crack into the hanging dihedral and follow this to its termination (A3, some 6°). A pitch of scrambling up and leftwards takes one to the foot of the Great Flake. Suggested bivi number two (15 pitches from foot of wall).

FRENCH DESCRIPTION. UPPER WALLS

Stage 3. Move up right by a chimney to a ledge at the foot of a hidden diedre. Ascend this (5° A1, loose) left of the great black stripes. Continue left and up by hard artificial pitches (A2, A3, A4, some free) with a deviation right and back left to a small diedre. Climb the diedre (A2, A3) over two small overhangs to a rope length (A3) over the Big Overhangs (peg in situ by a dangerously loose block – do not touch). From a belay in etriers continue over overhangs (A2) onto the Summit Wall. About six days.

Stage 4. Still on steep rock continue up, then right for about two rope lengths (6°, A1) then a pitch over an overhang (A2). Trend right again then more or less straight up (6°, A1, A2) to a ledge. Here it may be possible to ascend directly to the summit. Failing this, make a traverse out right (5°sup) followed by a rope length up to the left edge of the Summit Gully on the English Route. This edge is then followed to the West Ridge and summit.

162. THE ESCAPE TRAVERSE
(D Pearce and E Ward Drummond. 1969)

Approx 200m, with one pitch of A2.

From the foot of the Great Flake walk left along ledges to where they peter out. An abseil takes one down to a ledge from where a pitch of A2 up the central of three obvious grooves leads to the 90m pinnacle which is detached from the face and easily seen. A troglodyte pitch among the boulders behind this brings one to a further ledge system. Another 60m of scrambling suffices to reach the East Pillar Route, at the base of the Summit Gully.

163. THE FRENCH DIRECT – POLISH VARIANT
(M Kesicki, R Kowalewski, W Kurtyka, T Piotrowski. 17–19 Mar 1974)

The Polish Variant branches out of the original French line above the overhangs of the third wall (stage three) and goes across the final stretches of the Upper North Face. Grade VI sup.

Above the overhangs of the third wall climb a smooth slab, using a crack, 12m up to where the crack decays. Here, tension traverse leftwards over the edge of the slab to a shallow hollow. Then 25m up to the bottom of the overhangs above (6°, A2). A diagonal traverse to the left on the very

edge of the overhangs (A2) to a shallow niche and stance. Then up a vertical small wall to a steep ramp (A1) rising up leftwards. Along the ramp onto a large terrace (40m). Above the terrace there rises the summit section of the North Face. From here up a narrow chimney (A1) to its end and a traverse rightwards to a stance at a chipped off flake. Then a few metres horizontally to the right and an abseil with a 5m pendulum onto a ledge below. Along the ledge rightwards (5°, A1) to the foot of a vertical diedre. 40m up the diedre (A2) loose rocks, then slightly to the right over the edge of the face (5°, A1) and upwards turning a bit to the right to the bottom of a small overhanging face. Up the face (A2) and then onto the summit ridge which is gained to the left of the summit.

164 THE RIMMON (ENGLISH) ROUTE
(A Howard, J Amatt, B Tweedale. 1965)

Warning: *much of this route has been destroyed by a giant rockfall. This description is from the first ascent and is given for historical interest only.*

A long climb of continuous steepness, the natural route of 'The Wall' and a classic of its grade. It takes the easiest line through otherwise almost impenetrable overhanging walls and is a serious undertaking. The Exit Chimneys would be harder in adverse conditions and retreat from above the Great Wall is not easy. Mostly sustained free climbing on good rock, with some pitches of artificial. Above the Great Wall etriers are not essential though some parties may prefer them on the Narrow Slab. All pegs and wedges (including those for belays) were left in place on the first ascent (approx 100 pegs and 25 wedges for aid). The time on the first ascent was 5½ days (78 climbing hours).

Recommended bivouac sites are the First Bivouac, the Central Basin and the Summit Gully. These are the most likely places to find snow or water which may present a problem after July. Stonefall was non-existent. It is usually climbed now (1970) in two or three days from the valley (about 24 climbing hours from the First Bivouac) but has been done in a single 18 hour day. 1,200m. Grade VI sup. Photos and Diag pgs 88, 91 and below.

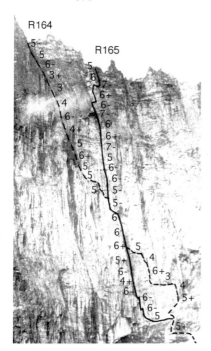

The route was first climbed free in 1979 by H C Doseth and R Amundsen with three pitches of Norwegian 6+ (English 5c). The best times in 1997 were down to 10–20 hours, though it had been done in less than 8! See Klatring i Romsdal. The first winter ascent was 4–13 Mar 1976 by V Sirl, M Smid, J Janis, P Plachecky and J Raconcaj. The following description was from the first ascent:

From Fiva Farm ascend through birch woods and up scree and snow slopes to the foot of the Introductory Wall at the back of the amphitheatre (2–4 hours). Cross the bergschrund from the right and traverse a ramp to the centre of the buttress (60m, 3°). Ascend by zig-zags for 75m (5°, one pitch 5° A1) then trend left up easy rock and snow for 60m. Now, depending on snow conditions, either ascend the snowfield diagonally towards its top left, or move left near its base between seracs on steep slabs (30m, 6°) to the undercut base of the wall. Follow this, sometimes on steep snow or, in the late season, by easy scrambling on its left, for 60m (4°) almost to the head of the snowfield. Cross the bergschrund and ascend the undercut groove for 30m (5°, A1) or, if the snow is too far from the wall, ascend the slanting groove about 10m left of this (6°, peg) to the First Bivouac. Snow and water at the bottom of the previous pitch; 4 hours from start.

From the bivouac, move left on ledges for almost 60m (5°) to the base of a huge grey diedre – The Nick – and ascend it for 6m. Continue by the left wall for 45m (A2, A3 or, with pegs in place, A1), escaping free round the left arête in an exposed position. Move easily up to a ledge above The Nick (9m, 4°, loose rock) and ascend the left-hand crack in the wall behind (15m, 5°sup, pegs) to larger ledges; traverse easily left to a platform below the Great Wall. Bivouac site, possibly with snow. 6–8 hours from start.

Climb the short wall behind the bivouac (peg) and traverse left to gain another smaller ledge (peg, 24m, 6°). Tension down into the groove and gain the crack line in the Great Wall which is followed for almost 120m moving left below the overhanging prow (A2, 6° A1, 6° A1, A3 or, with pegs in place 6° A1), to a stance just below its upper edge. Escape from the Great Wall and traverse left for 24m (5°sup, 4°) to the base of an overhanging chimney – the Black Cleft. Ascend this (24m, 5°inf) moving left at the top, loose rock. Exit with difficulty (6°) to ledges which are followed easily left. A short crack (12m, 4°) leads to a better ledge: bivouac site, possibly with water.

Climb the Flake Crack above strenuously for 30m (6°, peg) then move left past an extremely large loose block and up a short awkward crack (6°). Easier climbing trending left (3°) leads to the back of the Central Basin. Ascend a short crack (4°) to an ideal bivouac site at the foot of the Narrow Slab. Snow usually available at the back of the basin until mid season or later.

Ascend the Narrow Slab which cuts a superb line through the overhangs, mainly by its inner edge for 60m, moving left below roofs, then up and back right to a sensational prow above them (5°inf, loose, 6° pegs). Follow the steep groove above for 30m (6°) to a small ledge on the right. Bivouac site.

Continue up the groove (24m, 6°) to the foot of the overhanging Exit Chimney at the level of the Big Overhangs on the French Direct. Ascend the Chimneys, normally wet, for 90m (6° pegs) to the base of the Summit Gully. More easily now, follow the Gully, mainly on the left side for about 165m (4°sup) passing snow, water, and two possible bivouac places to a point where the Gully steepens and splits into two cracks. Take the left-hand crack for 75m (5°sup, 6° pegs, 5°) to a ledge, bivouac site; snow.

Traverse back into the Gully and ascend steep snow for 15m (3°) to below a huge chockstone. Ascend through a hole behind (5°) or, in the very early season it is possible to gain its top directly from the snow. A slab and groove now lead left for 24m (5°sup) to a small roof. Escape by overhangs on the right and climb up to a col on the West Ridge (12m, 5°). Easy climbing up the ridge leads to the summit.

165. THE SWEDISH ROUTE (TROLLGUBBEN ROUTE)

(L G Johansson, T Hilsson. 17–20 Jun 1978. First winter ascent, H C Doseth, K Svanemyr, H Nesheim. Feb 1979. First free ascent, H C Doseth, S Bancroft, C Brooks. 1980)

Warning: *much of this route has been destroyed by a giant rockfall. This description is from the first ascent and is given for historical interest only.*

This was the second most popular route on The Wall until the big 1998 rockfall which destroyed much of it. When it was first climbed, it made a rather direct connection between the Introductory Wall and the pinnacle called 'Gubben' or 'Trollgubben' This description is from the first ascent: the route joins the Rimmon Route for the Great Wall and Black Cleft. From there it continues straight up to the big triangular roof clearly seen from below, which is passed to the right. Somewhat complicated route finding gives a finish at Gubben. A classic. 1,200m. Grade VI sup. Diags pgs 97, 99.

The climbing is mostly free with a few pitches of 4° but otherwise Grade 5° and 6°. Longer artificial sections are found on the 'Grey Wall' (Pitches 16 and 17). On many other pitches artificial moves are mixed with the free climbing. The aid climbing is never harder than A2. For comparison, the route is more sustained than the American Direct on the West Face Direct of the Drus.

Good bivouac sites are: 1. Just below Great Wall, Rimmon Route (Pitch 7). 2. 20m above the Black Cleft (Pitch 12). 3. On the Terrace (Pitch 14). 4. A good ledge three pitches from the top (Pitch 23). Compare with the topo, on which the pitches are numbered P1, P2 etc. Numbers located at the top of each pitch.

The route now goes free and is climbed in 15–30 hours with three pitches of Norwegian 7- (English 6a). For additional topo see Klatring i Romsdal.

The following description is from the first ascent:

To find the start, climb the Introductory Wall as for Rimmon Route. Then traverse immediately on to the base of the wall proper, over the lower part of the snowfield (or later in the summer below the snow).

1. The first pitch on the wall leads by a diagonal traverse from the right to small ledges below an orange coloured overhanging wall, easily seen from below.
2. Climb the obvious crack to the left and traverse left into a corner which is followed until it ends with a roof. Traverse left, with difficulty, to stance.
3. Fix a high point and make a pendulum to the left into the next corner, which is climbed. A groove leads to a good stance.
4. Traverse again to the left and climb another corner. One is now situated at the foot of the huge corner where the Great Wall forms the upper left-hand side.
5/7. Climb the corner for 130m up to 5m under a triangular roof (P5, P6, P7). Here the Rimmon Route is joined (traverse on to the left wall and follow cracks). A good bivouac site is found 20m to the right of the foot of the wall.
8/12. The Rimmon Route is followed until above the Black Cleft (P8–P12). Possible bivouac site.
13/14. Starting 15m to the right of the beginning of the Flake Crack, follow cracks and corners (often wet), which are vertical continuations of the Black Cleft, to reach a big sloping ledge, the Terrace (90m). P14 has an awkward artificial start but ends with a beautiful clean curving jam-crack. Bivouac site on the Terrace.
15/20. One is now standing at the bottom of the Grey Wall, a vertical 200m high, compact surface which is terminated by a huge triangular roof 'the Big Roof'. The Wall is climbed first on broken rock (P15), then by cracks in smooth granite (in part artificially) up to within 10m of a smaller roof to the right of and below the big one (P16–P18). Traverse left into a sequence of small corners, which are followed upwards, passing the right-hand side of the Big Roof (P19, P20). Stop at blocks, where thin ledges lead out to the right.
21/22. Follow these ledges horizontally to the right to an arête, from where a pendulum can be done into the next corner (this is a key-passage). Climb the corner (a fine crack, straight as an arrow, the 'Troll Crack') up to an overhang (P21). Above the overhang is another corner (with a jammed, dangerous looking block) leading to ledges (P22). Traverse right 10m.
23/24. Now, don't climb the first promising corner (leads to a blank wall), but descend to a good ledge, possibly with snow. From the right-hand side of the ledge, climb a sharp corner up to a roof. Traverse right under the roof on to ledges (P24), (some artificial), situated precisely below the gap between Gubben and Kjerringa.
25/26. The final pitches start with a long

leftward ascending traverse over piles of big blocks and ends by pulling over a big square jammed block in a chimney whereupon it is possible to crawl through a tunnel to the south side of the wall, at the left (eastern) edge of Gubben. Other finishes are certainly possible.

166.

A new route was attempted in 1975 by Cathcart and Slaney, ascending grooves 10m left of the First Bivouac on the English Route. They gained about 500m, which involved about 200m (6°) and a few pegs to a large arched roof. A traverse and thin cracks (6°) followed by both more pegs and (6°) led to easier ground. The third day involved a crack, then a quartz traverse and bolts then move (6°) to good ledges. Little height was gained on the walls above, as the weather deteriorated and the attempt was abandoned. Bolts and abseil pegs were left in

Åndalsnes and Romsdal from Norafjell

place but the fixed ropes left at the Arch Traverse and Quartz traverse to facilitate a retreat were removed on the descent. Like other routes on the right side of The Wall, it is not recommended.

For details of other routes on The Wall, including two Russian Routes climbed in 1997, see *Klatring i Romsdal*.

To reach the top and appreciate its breath-taking views more easily, approach it from behind.

167. WEST RIDGE
(Party unknown)

Seldom used, except in descent as part of the Troll Ridge, 90m. Grade II.

From the Ordinary Route to Store Trolltind (Route 182) scramble up gullies and broken rock to the col between Trollspiret and Trollryggen, where the Rimmon Route used to emerge. Further scrambling follows on good but broken rock, about 15m right of the edge (some 2° or 3°, dependent on line).

168. DESCENT BY THE ORDINARY ROUTE

An easy scramble down the south west side passing the bivouac under Klumpen, and joining the Stigfoss path just before reaching the good boulder bivouac above Storgrovbotnen (about ½ hour). Total time down to the Stigfoss huts, about 2½ hours.

The next climbs are on the exposed pinnacles on the very top edge of the Troll Wall (diags pgs 88 and 93).

Trollspiret

169. EAST RIDGE
(M Hansen, A Naess. 1979)

This is the fine spire-shaped pinnacle on the Troll Ridge with a twin-peaked summit overhanging the Troll Wall. Grade II inf.

It is usually approached by descending the West Ridge of Trollryggen, then up from the col, or one may gain the col by scrambling up broken gullies from the Ordinary Route to Store Trolltind.

Trollgubben

170. SOUTH EAST FACE
(O Broch, E Fjeld. 1926)

This (when approached from the south) is the right-hand of two famous Troll pinnacles, the petrified 'Old Man's Face' looking out over The Wall. There is a choice of several routes from this side, the easiest beginning on the right. About 60m. Grade II.

From high up on the snow (or scree) ascend leftwards to the gap on spacious ledges. Turn left of another pinnacle, then exposed climbing to the top.

Trollkjerringa

This, 'The Old Woman' is the most renowned of the Troll pinnacles and her face can be seen staring out over Romsdal to the left of 'The Old Man'.

171. SOUTH FACE
(E Kierulf, L Onsanger. 1941)

The route to Store Trolltind passes just beneath the south face of the pinnacle. About 90m. Grade III sup

Ascend for a couple of pitches by the right-hand side, moving left to finish up the ridge proper.

172. SOUTH EAST SIDE
(A B Bryn, D B Purchardt, N Nygaard, E and L Sundt. 1916)

This is the easiest route on 'The Old Woman', and also the usual way of descent. About 60m. Grade III inf.

From the gap between Gubben and Kjerringa, go through a cleft in the right-hand side before moving left of a shoulder. Keep up and left onto a flat rock and up a short steep wall (difficult in descent) to easy rocks and the top.

173. WEST WALL
(A R Heen, H Berg, J Unghjem. 1941)

A short but steep route in an exposed position on the edge of Trollveggen. About 30m. Grade IV.

From the 'balanseblokka' (rocking stone) ascend on good holds, as directly as possible, passing a bulge at half height with difficulty.

174. SOUTH WEST WALL
(P Livesey, A N Other. 1967)

The route starts from a point beneath the col at the foot of the West Wall. Grade V.

Climb the steep wall via the obvious crack, passing a small overhang above which the angle eases.

Brurjentene

175. SOUTH EAST SIDE

The next pinnacles along the ridge are reached easily from the south east. Grade I.

Brura

The old Brura was climbed in 1882 by Hall, Soggemoen and Norahagen, but most of it collapsed over the Troll Wall in 1946 leaving the present sharp needle.

176. SOUTH EAST SIDE
(A R Heen, M Borg, G Malones. 1947)

Short, with few difficulties. Grade IV inf.

Brur Skar

This is the lowest gap on the ridge and a renowned viewpoint with a sensational vertical drop of 900m down the Troll Wall. Definitely worth the walk – especially if you are a base jumper about to jump off!

177.

Brur Skar is passed on the Ordinary Route (Route 182) to Store Trolltind. 3–4 hours. Grade I.

Brudgommen

178. SOUTH WEST SIDE
(C Hall, J Venge, M Soggemoen. 1882)

This is the big pinnacle between Brur Skar and Store Trolltind and is easily reached from the Ordinary Route to the latter. Grade II.

Scramble up the gullies beyond Brur Skar and turn right near the top to reach the summit. Like Brur Skar a good viewpoint for the Trollveggen climbs.

179. EAST PILLAR
(M Glogoczowski, M Kozlowski, A Paulo. 1968)

The main feature of the route is the pillar forming the extreme right edge of the Troll Wall basin, and the left edge of Fiva Couloir. On the first ascent it was approached from the cwm under the wall but it may be reached more quickly and easily via Fiva Route. The route gives good climbing in fine situations and escape is possible at half and three-quarters height into Fiva. First climbed in two days, it is thought to be possible in one day for a competent rope of two. 1,350m. Grade V sup.

The climb starts on the south face of Brudgommen a rope length above the first slabs which cross the cwm below the Troll Wall and approximately level with the start of the French Direct.

Climb for three pitches (2°, 3°) up slabs and grassy shelves to the short chimney in the vertical walls. After the chimney (3°) bear slightly right across small walls and ledges to an edge leading left. A vertical wall (5°sup) follows and brings one to easy angled slabs above a small snowfield. From this point, two parallel chimneys cutting the wall of Brudgommen are visible. Approach by slabs for two pitches (2°, 3°) and then climb by the right edge of the right chimney (5°, one place A1) to the pillar. One is now above the hanging snowfield on Fiva Route and this point can be reached easily from that route.

Follow the sharply defined ridge (3°, 4°sup) to a ledge and large flat stone where it abuts against a vertical wall. (Snow and water in gully below to right). Ascend the right edge of the wall until it is possible to return left (5°, 6°). Continue slightly left by a steep wall and grassy shelves to the right-hand chimney on the left of the pillar. Ascend this to the yellow overhanging band of rocks and traverse horizontally right along a ledge with loose blocks to the large ledge on the nose of the pillar. (This is six pitches above the 'flat stone' – bivouac recommended.)

Now ascend by a system of walls (4°, 5°) and easy ledges up the right side of the pillar (the left flank of Fiva Couloir) until the wet chimney is reached leading to the gap between Brudgommen and Ugla Pinnacle. Some metres up the chimney it is possible to traverse left for one and a half rope lengths (4°) to regain the nose of the pillar. Two more pitches up huge steps on the ridge (6°, 5°) lead to the summit.

Ugla

180. SOUTH SIDE
(M Hansen, A Naess. 1929)

This is the strange looking pinnacle left of the col under the south ridge of Store Trolltind. For obvious reasons it is called The Owl. Grade II.

Spørsmålstegnet

181. SOUTH SIDE
(Party unknown. About 1929)

This pinnacle 'The Question Mark', is a sharp needle between Ugla and Store Trolltind. Grade II sup.

Store Trolltind 1,795m (5,888ft)

Obvious from Åndalsnes from where the still unclimbed North Face is easily seen.

182. ORDINARY ROUTE
(C Hall, M Soggemoen, J Venge. 1882)

A long, easy and very worthwhile mountain scramble, passing the famous sensational Brur Skar view point at the top of the Troll

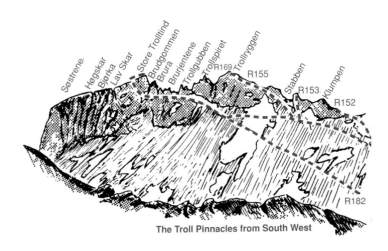

The Troll Pinnacles from South West

Wall. Once into the first hanging valley the whole of the route can be snow covered in the early season, but with no real scrambling until beyond Brur Skar. Although the way is still quite well cairned beyond here inexperienced parties may have some difficulties in route finding through the final complex system of ridges and gullies where the easiest way is not always obvious. 3–4 hours to Brur Skar. (No technical difficulties to here other than some rising traverses on snow where axes can be useful.) 4–5 hours from the start to the summit. Grade II inf.

From the viewing place above the Stigfoss waterfalls, ascend leftwards across a slab. This may be avoided by walking round to the right from near the top of the steps. A well trodden path then contours north eastwards round the rim of Isterdal before rising up by the side of a waterfall into the first hanging valley.

Cross the river (snow or boulders) and follow cairns up scree or snow slopes north eastwards to the saddle under the west ridge of Breitind; large cairn. Continue in a similar direction along the northern side of the upper hanging valley (frozen lakes and much snow for most of the season). Here, there are two ways – either along the slabby ridge above Storgrovbotnen or, lower, along the shoulder above the frozen lakes. There is a bivouac (usually snow-covered) on this lower path. Either way brings one to the saddle

above Storgrovbotnen with a large boulder moraine and a good bivouac site.

Now, gaining a little height, bear left on scree or snow with the pinnacles of Klumpen and Stabben high above, and then horizontally by a cairned track of broken rocks and snow slopes beneath the southern buttresses of Trollryggen and Trollspiret. Beneath Kjerringa and Gubben the track becomes much more pronounced and may well be called 'The Troll's Highway' until suddenly it reaches the breathtaking gap of Brur Skar.

From the Skar, continue below the southern buttress of Brudgommen along the cairned track to the skyline, and then ascend gullies (some 2°) until the col of Ugla Skar is reached above Fiva Couloir. Go through a hole in the ridge and ascend by further gullies, keeping left at most obstacles (some 2°) reaching the summit plateau west of the top. The final ridge may be taken direct on good rock (2°sup). Good little hut on the summit. (If one continues too far left before ascending the gullies one exits up a deep snow gully to Lav Skar – the deep notch on the West Ridge. The ascent from here is 4° or, easier, up a gully on the right (2°).

183. WEST RIDGE
(C Lysholm, H Nygaard. 1922)

Hardly used except for descent. There is very little actual climbing and the approach is long. 8 hours from Sogge. Grade III inf.

A fairly well-marked path leaves the road 100m or so north east of the road junction near the cabins of Moen Motel. It zig-zags steeply up through trees past a pylon and, above the tree line, follows the northern side of Oraabotnen to the top of Norafjell. The direction is now approximately south east across Adelsfjell and Adels Glacier until below Midtre Trollklørne. Possible danger from crevasses. (4–5 hours.) Cross the bergschrund and ascend slabby wet rock to the south col, then up without difficulty to the north west plateau which curves easily round above the glacier to the first gap – Høg Skar.

Descend into the Skar, and climb out by its north west wall or, easier, descend a little to the south and then up by a little gully near Bjørka needle. Continue along the plateau and scramble down into the next gap – Lav Skar. Escape from Lav Skar by its west wall (4°) or go down a rope length to the south and back up by a gully. It is then an easy walk to the top.

184. HØG SKAR
(H C Bowen, C W Patchell. 1903)

Seldom used, the route goes up the right-hand of the two great snow couloirs on the north face. 6 hours. Grade III inf.

Follow Route 183 onto Adelsbreen which is crossed to the foot of the couloir – some crevasses. Cross the bergschrund (this can be difficult after mid season) and ascend the snow-filled couloir for about 180m to the Skar. From then on, the route is as for 183.

185. LAV SKAR
(R Bicknell, E Norahagen. 1894)

Viewed from Adelsbreen in the north, this is the left-hand, and longest, of the two great snow couloirs and forms the right edge of the north face proper. Seldom used, except in descent. 6 hours. Grade III.

Follow Route 183 onto Adelsbreen which is crossed to the foot of the couloir – some crevasses possible. Cross the bergschrund (this can be diffiult after mid season) and ascend the wide snow-filled couloir for about 240m to the Skar, where Route 183 is rejoined.

186. NORTH EAST RIDGE
(E Fjelde, S Suhrke. 1927)

A long approach but once on the ridge the climbing is good, situated between the 300m north wall and the 1,500m East Face with superb views of the Troll Wall. 6 hours from Sogge. 300m. Grade IV inf.

Take Route 183 to Adelsbreen then easily onto the northern continuation of the ridge. Follow this above the glacier and over the top of Nordre Trolltind to the start of the ridge proper where it steepens up the edge of the north face. This point may be reached directly, but with difficulty, from the glacier.

From here, pass a small pinnacle and move out right up two slabs to a large block. Now,

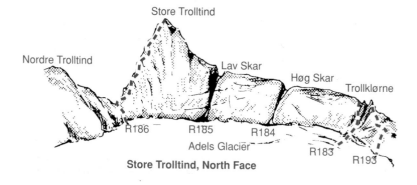

Store Trolltind, North Face

with greater difficulty, continue up on small holds and up a sloping groove to the right for a rope length. Easier climbing brings one to scree slopes just right of the summit.

Next, approaching from the depths of Romsdal is one of the area's first big routes:

187. EAST FACE, FIVA ROUTE
(A R Heen, E Heen. 1931)

A long introduction on very easy angled grassy slabs leads into the huge couloir under the south east wall. Difficulties in the couloir vary with snow conditions which can be alpine. There is some avalanche danger in the early season. A classic but long and consequently fairly serious route for its comparatively low grade. 5–9 hours. Over 1,800m. Grade IV inf. Diag pg 77.

An obvious rake slants diagonally across the East Face from right to left and is followed pleasantly enough for about 900m on very easy angled slabs (2°) with some grass and snow to the main couloir. Descend a little and cross the mouth of the couloir (steep snow) and continue still easily (2°) up its left edge until the rock steepens and narrows into a ridge. Climb the ridge or a narrow gully on the right for five to six rope lengths (3°, 4°) then cross onto a broad ridge on the left of the main couloir reaching it at a ledge below a small steep crag. Pass this on the right and follow the ridge for several rope lengths (3° and 4°) until it fades into the main left wall of the couloir. This, in turn, is followed often with snow and wet rock (3°, 4°) to a point where the gully splits. Gain the left branch by traversing in above a narrow chimney and then follow the dividing ridge (3°) until it leads into the exit chimney at the top left of the couloir. Escape through a hole under a chockstone onto the ridge at Ugla Skar (often heavily corniced in the early season). The Ordinary Route is then followed to the summit.

188. DESCENT BY THE ORDINARY ROUTE

Scramble south down gullies and follow the track to Stigfoss. Route 182 in reverse. 2¹/₂–3 hours.

189. DESCENT BY LAV SKAR

Climb down into the Skar (4°) and glissade almost to the mouth of the couloir (or, in the early season, straight onto the glacier). Abseil into the bergschrund and exit (possibly with difficulty) onto the glacier. Continue the descent by Adelsbreen and Route 183. About 2 hours.

190. DESCENT BY TROLLKLØRNE

Reverse Route 183 to the col under Søndre Trollklørne, from which take Route 193 in reverse, with or without inclusion of the Middle Claw. About 4 hours.

Søstrene

These are a group of sharp pinnacles on the south face of the summit plateau, west of Lav Skar. Prior to the 1980s, there were no routes on their south and west faces which are both quite long and fairly inaccessible. Hans Doseth put that right, climbing a route on each wall, see *Klatring i Romsdal*.

191.

Some were ascended by their shorter northern sides, approaching from the plateau in 1939 by E Birkenland, E H Falkenthal and S Hansen. Grade II.

Bjørka

192. NORTHERN SIDE
(A R Heen, J F Strømme. 1930)

This is the pinnacle just south of the gap of Høg Skar. Grade III. Diag pg 103.

Descend one rope length from the Skar to the gap at the foot of the pinnacle and ascend to its top by the right-hand side.

Trollklørne

193. NORTH RIDGE
(C and J Lysholm. 1912)

Seldom used, except in descent, the route passes from north to south over the three sharp Troll's Claws on the north west spur of Store Trolltind. 6 hours from Sogge. Grade III. Diag pg 104.

Follow Route 183 onto Adelsbreen and ascend slabby rock to the top of the Northern Claw (3°). Descend half a rope length and contour to the south col of Midtre which is climbed by its south ridge (3°). Easier climbing follows to the top of the South Claw.

Nordre Trolltind
1,618m (5,307ft)

194. NORTH RIDGE
(W Bromley-Davenport M P and J Venge. 1870)

Mostly used for descent. The summit has superb views of Romsdal and Trollveggen. 4 hours. Grade I. As for Route 186, which crosses over this peak.

Now, ascending from Romsdal once more, is:

195. SOUTH EAST RIDGE
(J Brown and T Patey. 1967)

A worthwhile route despite occasional vegetation and a long introduction up Fiva Route. The actual ridge gives good climbing though an easier gully line in the upper part

would, if taken, greatly diminish its importance. It is seen in profile from Fiva Farm and strikes up right from the hanging snowfield on Fiva Route. There is a shoulder at one-third height and a prominent unnamed tower at just over two-thirds. 7 hours. 1,650m. Grade V. Diag pg 108.

Scramble up Fiva Route (Route 187) for about 750m to the highest heather ledge on the corner. Attack the rib right of centre and then ascend diagonally leftwards by a system of grooves and cracks (4°) below a rock scar to reach easier ledges on the left flank. Continue up a grassy gully to a horizontal grass band. Tackle the frontal slab wall by the central crack. At 36m, traverse horizontally left by a large ledge and then climb straight up a shallow grooved gully for 54m (4°, 5°, some vegetation). The line is now more obvious and a further 150m (some 4°) on the left flank of the ridge above the hanging snowfield leads eventually onto the shoulder. This next section of the ridge is the key, and terminates in the huge square-cut tower 280m above. It would be possible to bypass this by a chimney-gully line well across to the left. Go three rope lengths up steep slabs left of the true crest (4°, 4°sup) to the base of a deep but well concealed chimney at least 90m high and packed with chockstones. Chimney work for four pitches (5°, 5°sup, 4°,

Descending the Ordinary Route from the Troll Pinnacles

4°), finishes with a tunnel exit into a jumble of huge blocks. Step right, off the highest block, and traverse very thinly around a holdless corner (5°sup) then continue straight up the east face of the tower, close to the edge. Two long exposed pitches of sustained difficulty (36m, 5°sup. 24m, 5°sup, one peg) lead to the top of The Tower.

From the col beyond The Tower it should be possible to finish directly up the 90m Terminal Wall. It is much easier to scramble up leftwards and finish in one pitch by the right-hand of twin cracks. This exits on the main ridge at a little col 36m below the summit.

196. EASTERN DIEDRE
(T Crosby, G Rawson, G Cullingham, K Leadbeater. 1966. Climbed free, G Chelton and D Wright. 1974)

As for the previous route, a long introduction up Fiva Route is followed by good climbing on the upper wall, which is tackled by the immense diedre leading to the col just south of the top. The diedre is steep and serious and, climbed free, there are two pitches of Norwegian 6+ (English 5c). Snow and water is available in the diedre. The first ascent took three days, with bad weather in the upper diedre. Future ascents should be possible in 1½ days. About 1,500m. Grade VI. Diag pg 108.

Follow Fiva Route to the snowfield and zig-zag rightwards over slabs (2°, 3°) to the large snowfield just left of the diedre. Bivouac site.

From the snowfield traverse right for 30m to the foot of a chimney and climb the rib on its left for 60m (3°sup). Continue by slabs and cracks for 120m (3°, 4°) to the foot of the tremendous grey diedre. Follow it for 15m (A2, 12 pegs) with an awkward move right onto a small ledge. Climb the wall above for 30m (5°) keeping left of a wet crack to a short, difficult overhanging corner (6m, 5°sup). Bivouac site.

Scramble 24m up to the next steep section of the diedre and follow the chimney for a rope length (4°) to a small sandy stance at the foot of a crack. Ascend this (18m, 5°)

followed by a loose wall on the left (18m, 5°), then a short awkward chimney (18m, 4°) to a large flake. Climb the steep slab on the left for 28m (5°) to a line of overhangs. Take the obvious line of weakness just left of the corner, passing an awkward overhang (18m, A2, 10 pegs) to a sloping grass ledge and tension traverse rightwards, back into the wide chimney. Bivouac site.

Follow the narrowing chimney for a rope length (4°) passing behind a large chockstone to a scree ledge below a wet cave. Climb into the cave and out by the left wall (28m, 4°) to a niche, then up the corner for 21m (3°) to a loose chockstone. Ascend a short overhanging corner with an awkward exit to the left (21m, 4°), above which 60m of easy angled slabs (2°) lead to the foot of the final steep section. Climb the corner to a small cave and then over dangerous flakes to a large ledge on the right wall (36m, 4°). Using a pinnacle on the left side of the ledge, surmount an overhanging corner and climb the crack above (18m, 5°sup). Traverse left for 15m to a good stance and then directly upwards for 8m (5°) to the top of the diedre. (Junction with the south east ridge). Scramble 45m leftwards and exit by a short steep crack (5°) to the col. A further pitch (3°) leads to the summit.

197. DESCENT BY THE ORDINARY ROUTE

Follow the ridge north, descending onto Adelsbreen and down Route 183 to Sogge. About 1½ hours.

198. EAST FACE
(Z Drilik and J Stejskal)

No description. 20 hours. Grade V. Diag pgs 108 and 109.

199. LEFT-HAND RIDGE
(D Barley and G Ward. 1971)

Between Nordre Trolltind and Adelsfjell is an unnamed peak. Below this on the eastern face is an amphitheatre with a gully draining out below. Down to the right of the gully is a sweep of white slabs. Initially the route ascends the white slabs, then the vegetation

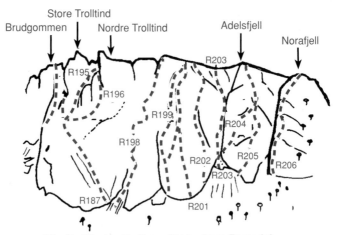

Store Trolltind
Brudgommen   Nordre Trolltind   Adelsfjell
Norafjell

R195
R196
R203
R199
R204
R198
R202
R205
R206
R203
R187
R201

The Trolltinder, Northern Peaks, from Romsdal

of the ridge right of the gully, and continues past a short pink wall and up the blunt ridge above (immediately right of the amphitheatre). It trends rightwards to finish on the shoulder. 1,100m. Grade V. Diag pg 109.

Start from the top of the scree cone and scramble 100m up the left edge of the white slabs. Go diagonally right (30m, 5°) across slabs, then up vegetated grooves trending leftwards to a clump of trees (230m, 3°inf, 4°). Ascend the vegetated ridge above to where the rock steepens (150m, 4°inf, 3° 2°). Climb up rightwards (50m, 4°), then leftwards to an A-corner (60m, 4°) which is passed by traversing the left wall (5°). Continue directly up to below the left corner of the pink wall (100m, 4°). Move left and climb a steep chimney (5°) and up right to the 'Pink Oval' (50m). Climb grooves trending left to the base of a black slanting corner just visible from the Pink Oval (70m, 5°). Climb a flake into this corner, but then ascend a small groove on the left (30m, 5°). Ascend cracks, above and go up right across the wall to the top of the slanting corner (30m, 5°). Climb up ribs and gullies trending rightwards to the shoulder (200m, 4°, 3°, 2°) (8 hours).

After half an hour's scrambling contour right above the Eastern Couloir and descend via Route 124.

200. DIESKA ROUTE
(J Dieska and P Dieska. 1973)

No info. 17 hrs. GradeVI. Diags pgs 108, 109.

201. CENTRAL RIDGE
(T and R Barley 1971)

No info. 900m. Grade IV. Diags pgs 108, 109.

202. HAZUCHA ROUTE
(J Hazucha and R Messo. 1973).

17 hrs. Grade V sup, A2. Diags pgs 108, 109.

203. EASTERN COULOIR
(A Howard and W Gartside. 1967)

The route lies up the left flank of the great couloir defining the northern limit of the east face of Nordre Trolltind. The crux is dangerous and difficult and the upper half is, in summer, mostly scree. On the first ascent in spring, the whole of the upper section was a vast snowfield with an exit on steep ice. NOT RECOMMENDED. 9–11 hours. About 1,000m. Grade VI. Diags pgs 108, 110

Scramble up the left rib of the couloir for 180m (3°) then steep grooves and across a slab for a rope length (5°sup). Another pitch up a chimney (4°) leads to an overhanging

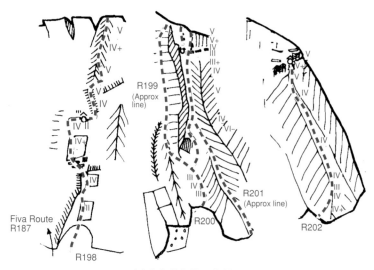

Adelsfjell & Norafjell

diedre. The diedre is extremely loose (6°sup, pegs, dangerous). From its top, move out easily right into the couloir (2°) and follow it for about 210m (3°, snow on first ascent). A further 210m (3°, snow on first ascent) up the left flank of the couloir leads to two difficult exit pitches (5°, ice on first ascent). Easy scrambling leads onto Adelsfjell, near the foot of the glacier.

Descent by the Ordinary Route, down Route 183 to Sogge. About 1 hour.

Adelsfjell

This small top at the north end of the Trolltind massif throws down a ridge of excellent glaciated slabs:

204. SOUTH EAST CRACKS
(D Scott and T Wells. 1970)

A good training climb and well worth doing for the beautiful clean cracks splitting the wall. Approach from the Fiva Farm gate through the woods, and follow the watercourse that comes down the left side of the East Buttress of Adelsfjell. Start below the obvious 100m wall seen at the top of this side of the buttress. 500m, 9 hours. Grade V sup. Diag and photo pgs 108, 111.

Follow the left buttress of a shallow couloir for three rope lengths – some loose rock, (5°sup). Traverse right above the couloir and under loose overhanging rock (5°). Climb up over jutting blocks (5°inf) and scramble up 100m to below the wall undercut at its base. Gain access to the wall by climbing up left (5°) and then by traversing right and down with tension (6°inf).

Climb up a groove about 10m and belay. Use 3 pegs to reach a good crack. Follow this until it is possible to traverse out left into the prominent crack that splits the wall. Climb up a few metres and belay (5°sup). Continue a full rope's length to the overhangs at the top of the wall (5°sup). Climb the overhangs first on the left, then right and onto easier ground (5°inf). Follow the ridge to the top of the mountain.

205. EASTERN SLABS
(J Duff and J Brazington. 1970).

Approach from the Fiva Farm gate, through the woods, across a large meadow, then a watercourse leads to the foot of the buttress. 800m Grade V. Diag and photo pgs 108 and 111.

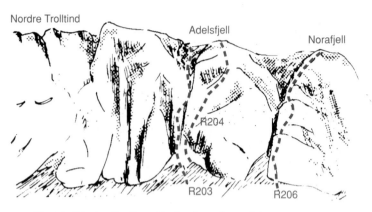

The Trolltinder, Northern Peaks, from Romsdal

Start from a grassy ledge 50–100m above the base of the slabs and about 60m below a large black cave, in an overlap, reached from right (via forest) or left (via ledges). Two pitches up to a ledge on the left of the obvious chimney-crack in the overlap (6°,4°). Move right into the crack (5°) and climb it (4°sup) to a stance above. Climb the belly of the slabs, bearing up left to the left end of the barrier (150m, pitches of 3°, 4°).

Climb across the steep wall on the left by ramps to a good flake belay (5°). Move round the corner on the left into a grassy pay, below a dirty gully. Ignore the gully and climb the wall on the right by a steep crack and corner (5°). From the stance traverse easily right along ledges above the barrier, past a copse to a depression, straight up from the belay (25m, 5°). Traverse right into a black crack on the nose and up this (45m, 5°). Up a large ledge (12m 3°) then up the wall behind and a groove leading right (4°). Follow the nose of the slabs directly by cracks and walls (pitches of 4°, 5°) with good ledges between, to the foot of the final wall. Climb out left to the foot of the wide winking crack, then up right to a grassy bay (4°). Climb the shallow black chimney above then move right into a steep crack. Up this (6°) to another grassy bay. Easier climbing leads to a birch-infested ledge and the end of the climb. Scramble to the top.

Descent down the Route 183 to Sogge. About 1 hour.

Norafjell 928m (3,044ft)

This is the northernmost summit of the massif and has some excellent routes on its glaciated slabs, with relatively easy access.

206. SOUTH EAST SPUR
(A Howard, R Holt. 1967)

The first route on the slabs. It follows the spur of slabs up the right edge of the great gully dividing Norafjell from the main east face of the Trolltinder. The rock is perfect throughout with interesting technical climbing. A good preparation for the bigger ridges. 5–8 hours, 600m, Grade V. Diags pgs 108 and above.

Start from trees, moving immediately onto good rock at the bottom left corner of the slabs and follow a groove (3°) which slants left through a steep wall to a terrace. Move left from the terrace (2°) onto the left skyline and nicely up slabs (3°) to a recess. Continue in the same line (3°) to the top of a rake. Ascend to the overhanging groove (5°) and the chimney and scramble up terraces to a huge grey slab. This is climbed near its centre for 21m (6°, 7 pegs), then a series of tension traverses right for 21m (6°, 3 pegs) before moving up and back left to a

good ledge. Continue along the ledge and escape with difficulty (5°) to a long corner. Follow this (2°), then out right and pleasantly up slabs (2°, 3°) for a further 150m, then an easy half hour's scramble to the top.

207. SOUTH EAST SPUR VARIATIONS

Takes the best way up the pillar (the way with most climbing).

Start up a black slab at the bottom of the pillar (3°) and continue up easily (3°) for 40m to a tree under a small overhang. Up this (4°) and straight up the grey slab above with a difficult move on the top (5°). Now take the cracks just to the right for 10m (6°inf) and leftwards on a good ledge. Then up an overhanging crack which is difficult at the start (6°) 15m. Then up an overhanging groove-chimney (4°sup) 20m and easy scrambling follows to the great slab. Here, continue by the first ascent route as above, or by:

208. VIA GRUNERO
(B Østigard, K Svanemyr, H Doseth. 1978)

Follows an impressive rightwards slanting crack. The start is to the left of a big detached flake up broken black rock (4°).

Then up an overhanging crack (6°) 35m. Continue up the beautiful crack for a full rope length (4°sup, 5°) to the top of the Great Slab.

209. FUTURE GAMES
(R Anderson, S Sandford, H Doseth. 1978)

A very fine route on good rock.

Starts from a tree approximately 40m to the left of 'Grunero'. First easy up broken rocks (2°) and up a small crack (3°sup) till it ends where the big one starts out right, 35m. Traverse right round a corner (5°inf) and up to some vegetation (5°) and rightwards to a ledge below where the crack starts to overhang, 35m. Up the crack and follow it – difficult and very sustained for 20m (6°sup).

Since these early routes these excellent slabs have had considerable development. Topos to the network of climbs are in *Klatring i Romsdal*.

Descent By abseil, or as for Route 183 down the north west shoulder to Sogge. About ³/₄ hour.

Now, moving round to the west side of the Trolltind massif, high above Isterdal, and on the west side of the Adelsbreen we come to:

Setergjeitind

210. SOUTH WEST PILLAR
(A Gruner, B Østigard. 1975)

The route starts from Isterdalssetta in Isterdalen. A long introduction up steep forest leads to enjoyable scrambling on the pillar above. 900m, Grade II.

Storgrovfjell 1,618m (5,307ft)

211. SOUTH EAST RIDGE
(Party unknown)

The summit is seldom visited but provides magnificent views of the Trolltind and Kongen groups. The method of ascent is up the South East Ridge from the Stigfoss–Store Trolltind path. Grade I.

Stigfoss Veggen

This is the rock wall boxing in the southern end of Isterdal with its famous Stigfoss waterfalls and spectacular hairpin-road of Trollstigen. Taking a more direct line up the wall is the next route:

212. WEST GULLY, KEN'S ROUTE
(K and R Stannard, D Little, W Gartside. 1967)

The route is named in memory of Ken Stannard, who lost his life in an accident on the East Face of Bispen later in the season of 1967. It follows a line up the left wall of the gully which is itself 100m or so left of the minor waterfall. About 5 hours. 540m. Grade V.

WARNING: These notes are from the first ascent. Since then there has been a rockfall just over halfway up the route.

Scramble up the scree cone, from near the hairpin bend and begin with a rope length up the left side of the gully (6°), followed by a second pitch up slabs (4°). Now, move slightly left, then straight up slabs (6°) to a small ledge then 33m (6°) first by a groove in the slabs for 24m, then delicately left beneath a bulge. Continue straight up for 90m (4°, 6°, greasy in wet conditions), then a

further rope length (4°) regains the gully beneath a cave. Traverse right for 45m (3°), then move round a corner and up towards a ramp (36m 3°). Up this back into the gully (45m 4°), finishing by moving onto a ledge and up right to the top (36m 3°).

Descent. The climb finishes level with the top of the Trollstig hairpin road and it is a simple matter to contour round and join the track down from the Trolltinder which leads to the souvenir shops above the main waterfall.

Stighorn (Stigbotnhorn) 1,583m (5,224ft)

The pyramidal west face of Stighorn dominates the skyline south east of Trollstigen and is approached easily over scree and rock from the Trollstig souvenir shops. There are good views of the Trolltind and Kongen groups from the summit.

213. NORTH WEST COULOIR
(K Gottmann and party. 1963)

No real difficulties, though the quality of the climb is dependent on snow conditions which usually improve towards the end of the season. Good views from the summit. About 3 hours. 600m. Grade II. Diag pg 114.

From the bottom of the face, follow the leftward slanting snow couloir for almost 300m onto the north ridge. Scrambling up the ridge then leads to the top.

214. WEST WALL
(A Howard, B Tweedale. 1967)

Very enjoyable climbing throughout; the route starts almost at the centre of the base where a prominent rock overlap sloping up right and a grassy ramp sloping up left, meet to form a V. From then on, the route moves left at almost all difficulties until the black stripes are reached high up. A long leftward traverse under white overhangs leads to the final wall. 6–7 hours. 600m. Grade V inf. Diag and photo pgs 113, 114.

Approach the face from the Stigfoss huts and

R214 R215

solo easily up the grass ramp for about 60m until below a black wall (block belays). Traverse right and over a rib onto grey slabs (5°inf) and follow them trending left through grooves to a platform. Continue straight up a steep wall (5°inf) and slabs above, to a recess. A pitch of awkward climbing follows rising up left to a terrace (5°) with a 6m flake on the wall above. Gain the flake with difficulty from the right (6°) then bear left up a groove to a ledge. From the right end of the ledge, ascend the steep wall (5°) and trend slightly left again up grooved slabs to a good rock platform. From its left end go straight up the right side of a rock-fall scar for a rope length (3°).

Now, traverse pleasantly right until the black stripes are reached and it is possible to move up easily and back left to a belay ledge with white overhangs above. Avoid the roofs by following the ramp up left until 3m from its top then make an exposed leftwards traverse (5°), then straight up a steep rock tower on excellent holds to another ledge. Follow the obvious groove above, leftwards to a chimney on the skyline (3°). Up this and a pitch up good slabs (3°), then up a short wall to the top.

215. WEST COULOIR
(O D Enersen and party. 1961)

The route starts at the same point as the previous climb and moves up to gain the great central couloir which gives some good climbing. 6–7 hours 600m. Grade IV sup. Diag pg 114.

Traverse right as for the West Wall, from the block belays at the start, and move over the rib onto the grey slabs (5°inf). Now, follow fault lines trending slightly rightwards up the face until at the foot of the couloir (mostly 4°sup). The route then follows the 240m rock couloir to the summit, the initial rope length (5°inf) being as hard as any.

216. SOUTH WEST BUTTRESS
(A Howard, K Chadwick. 1968)

A straightforward start up the South West Couloir and the prominent chimney above lead to harder climbing on the upper wall, in a fine position. Route finding is not easy. About 7 hours. 600m. Grade V. Diag pg 114.

Ascend the South West Couloir for about 120m (good 40° snow for most of the season) until below the prominent chimney. Climb this for 60m (3°, 2°) to a cave and snow patch, keeping mainly to the left wall. Continue by the same line for a further 90m (2°, 3°) mainly by grooves in the left edge of the chimney until the wall steepens.

Ascend a flake crack (4°) to a good ledge then make a long and awkward leftward traverse descending to a ledge formed by a detached block (6°inf). Go left again to a hidden groove which leads to steep chimneys and a leaning wall (6°inf) above which is a large sloping ledge beneath a white wall. Escape left from here in an exposed position (5°, loose) to gain a platform. Ascend a groove from the left end of this (5°) followed by a chimney to another sloping ledge beneath a white wall. Escape left again by a difficult exposed groove (6°).

Do NOT continue up the obvious steep corner above; instead traverse left with difficulty on steep exposed rock moving up to a small ledge (6°). This is the crux of the route and the key to the exit. From the back of the ledge take a steep chimney in the left wall (4°) then left a little and up by grooves to the top of a detached block (3°). Left of this a good crack cuts through a steep wall (4°sup), then a pitch of steep grooves and chimneys leads to the top.

217. SOUTH WEST COULOIR
(Party unknown)

A pleasant scramble to the summit, usually giving a little snow climbing. 2–3 hours. 600m. Grade II sup. Diag pg 114.

Climb the couloir on the lower right of the face. Until late summer, this is often mostly snow up to 40°, with some rock, until it exits after about 180m onto the South West Ridge. Up this to the summit choosing the most amenable line.

218. DESCENT BY THE ORDINARY ROUTE

Follow the east ridge to the first col, then make an almost direct descent of the south side into Alnesdal (often by a 600m glissade, up to mid season). Return west and north by the lake and riverside to the bridge at the Trollstig huts. About l hour.

219. THE STIGHORN–BREITIND–TROLLTIND RIDGE

This ridge system covers most of the summits in the Trolltind group and, depending on the choice of route, can be varied from Grade II sup to IV sup. The following description gives the easiest route which provides an excellent, though long day in the mountains. Most parties will require about 14 hours. Grade II sup.

Ascend to the summit of Stighorn by the North West Couloir (II, snow). Follow the ridge east, then north east to the top of Breitind which is descended easily northwards, over Søndre Trolltind to the south east ridge of Trollryggen. Follow this, over Klumpen and Stabben (II) and descend the West Ridge (II) to the col. Now, either scramble down the gullies to join the Ordinary Route to Store Trolltind, or include any of the Troll Pinnacles.

From the summit of Store Trolltind, descend via the pinnacles of Trollklørne (III) or, if time is pressing, via Lav Skar taking care at the bergschrund. Either way brings one to Adels Glacier and the descent via Norafjell.

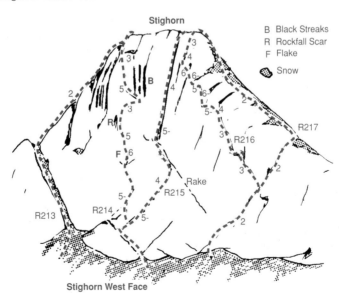

Stighorn

B Black Streaks
R Rockfall Scar
F Flake

Snow

R217
R216
R215
R214
R213
Rake

Stighorn West Face

The Kongen Group

Bispen, Kongen and Dronninga from Isterdal

The west side of the Isterdal valley is flanked for the whole of its 13km by this ridge of summits. Halfway along the ridge is a low pass, Urkleiva, over which is a track from Innfjord to Isterdal, a distance of 6.5km. North of here, the peaks are smaller, and the rock is much more broken and vegetated than on the majestic peaks to the south.

Here is a very famous trio of peaks – Bispen, Kongen and Dronninga (The Bishop, The King and The Queen). The climbs on Bispen are, in general, the easiest and most accessible, being situated immediately above the final hairpin of the Trollstig road, with the Stigfoss souvenir huts at its base. Kongen and Dronninga both present walls about 1,500m in height to the Isterdal valley and Kongen also has excellent climbing on its south wall which is very steep. All the big routes on these peaks are approached from the Isterdal road whilst the Ordinary Routes and south face climbs are approached from Stigfoss. There is a small bivouac hut on the summit of Kongen (in the north west corner) though it may be snow-covered until mid season. There is also a natural tunnel through the south ridge of Kongen just beneath the top, which provides good shelter. The only other constructed bivouac site in these peaks is in the boulders on the col between Bispen and Kongen.

There is accommodation in, and near to the entrance of, Isterdal at three camping sites all with huts, whilst Hotel Aak is just over the Rauma bridge on the Romsdal road towards Åndalsnes and has a good view of the valley. There is a bus route up Isterdal from Åndalsnes, (about 1½ hours to the top of Stigfoss) and on over the pass to Valldal. The road is not normally opened until the end of May, when the first snow ploughs are usually driven over the pass, carving a way between walls of snow sometimes 10m high! Assuming adequate snow, ski championships are held here, on the slopes south of the Bispen, on the first weekend in June.

There are also some good mountain walks in this area, one of the most popular being:

220. THE KLØVSTIEN TRAIL

This increasingly popular walk follows the old Trollstig pack-horse and cattle drover's road of Kløvstien. This ancient trail was first recognised as a 'highway' in 1766 and resurrected in the 1990s. As you make your way up or down the chain-protected cliffs within the spray of the Stigfoss Falls, think about the farmers that used to bring cattle down to the Romsdal Fair! It is said that one farmer lost 47 cattle here, having tied them together for the descent of the cliffs. 2 or 4km dependent on choice of route.

Once above the falls, sections of the old trail have been identified all the way to Valldal but most people will simply walk it either from its lower Isterdal junction with the road (about 4km) or from the car park below the falls (2km). Take care, the rocks are always wet by spray from the falls, and are consequently slippery. It wouldn't be a good place to fall from as the roaring chasm is just below!

Descending the route, the path (initially chained) starts just up the road from the bridge which dramatically spans the falls. After a steep descent on wet rock, the angle eases and the path continues down into Isterdal with unusual views of the winding hairpin bends of the road opposite. Take the first turn right to reach the lower car park, or continue through the woods with Kongen, then Dronninga above to the left, to meet the road lower down the valley

In ascent, either start from the car park below the falls, meeting the trail just after crossing the river, or start from the car park with the Kløvstien information board, which is 3km lower down Isterdal, about 3km after the second bridge over the Istra River on the E63 approaching from Romsdal.

Other walks in this massif include one which crosses the range:

221. ISTERDAL TO INNFJORD

A fairly short walk between the two valleys. About 8km.

About 5km up the Isterdal road from its junction with the main Romsdal road, and 2km after the second Istra River bridge is a signed track west to Isterdal Seter. Follow this and take the path past the seter up to Urkleiva, the obvious pass with pylons between Karitind and Svartbottstind (2km). Pass the little lake and follow the valley down to Innfjord.

Now, getting back on the rocks, high above the Stigfoss falls is the pyramidal peak of:

Bispen 1,475m (4,838ft)

222. SOUTH WEST FACE, ORDINARY ROUTE
(C Hall, M Soggemoen, E Norahagen. 1882)

An easy scramble mostly on scree. 2–3 hours from Stigfoss. Grade I.

From the Stigfoss tourist huts and car park go almost directly up the hillside and through a small cliff by an open gully (marker stone above). Continue up the hillside (some snow) then contour left beneath the south ridge to a prominent scree gully beyond. Follow the gully up onto the western side which is taken to the top (a little scrambling).

223. SOUTH RIDGE
(A R Heen, T Krohn. Winter 1932)

A pleasant and easy route to the summit. 2–3 hours from Stigfoss. Grade II inf.

Approach the south ridge as for the previous route and move up on cairned ledges to its foot. Follow the broad back of the ridge by shallow chimneys and broken rocks (2° loose) to a spacious platform. Climb a small wall above either directly (3°) or by corners to its right (2°) and continue more easily until a knife-edge ridge is crossed beyond which is the top.

224. EASTERN COULOIR
(Party unknown)

A route seldom used, having little climbing of real merit, but forms the approach for the

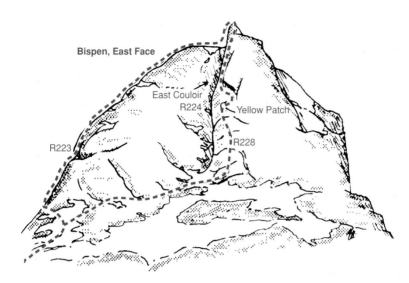

Bispen, East Face

East Couloir
R224
Yellow Patch
R223
R228

popular East Ridge routes. 3–4 hours from Stigfoss. 450m. Grade III.

From beneath the South Ridge go right and ascend a short way up glaciated slabs (2°). Go easily right across the slabs above snowfields until at the foot of the East Couloir (just over an hour). Continue still with little difficulty (2°, 3°) up the couloir for almost 120m to where the rock begins to steepen. The couloir is then followed directly to the col (some 3°sup) just south of the top.

225. SOUTH WALL, PHOENIX ROUTE
(P Livesey, J Stanger. 1967)

An enjoyable little route on steep rock. Technical difficulties are fairly hard for the grade but escape is possible from all belays either left into the East Couloir, or right onto the East Ridge. 3–4 hours. 450m. Grade IV sup.

As for the previous route cross the slabs (2°) and scramble up the couloir (2°, 3°) until level with the yellow patch on the East Ridge where the rock steepens. Now, traverse 12m right to the bottom of a slanting groove (3°). Ascend this for 45m (3°, 4°) to a belay, then up again (4°sup) onto slabs above. Ascend these to a flake belay below an overhanging V-shaped wall (3°), then go leftwards up a

gangway for 18m (4°) to a flake. Climb this (5°sup) and go up slightly left for 18m (4°) to a peg belay. Take slabs above before traversing left to the bottom of a steep corner (4°sup) and ascend this (peg) before moving left again and up a flake onto more slabs (6°). Climb the slabs for 9m and move left to a peg belay. Now a rope length straight up to the overhangs then left beneath them to a block belay (5°). A further 18m (4°sup) first over the overhang then up a groove on the left leads to the summit.

226. EAST RIDGE, ORIGINAL ROUTE
(A and S Gjendem, T Krohn. 1951)

Quite a pleasant route, but it avoids the better pitches on the Direct which are not much harder. 3 hours, 450m. Grade III inf.

Gain the East Couloir as above and after the second step move out onto the ridge by a break in its right wall (some 3°). Follow the slabby ridge easily (2°) to the platform under the Yellow Patch where the ridge is vertical.

Avoid the wall by a horizontal leftward traverse across the side wall to easier ground. Move up and back right a little (3°) to ledges on the ridge above the barrier. Continue by three or four pitches up cracks and chimneys in the left side of the ridge (3°) and finish by the short summit ridge.

227. GRABEINDIEDERET (GREY LEG CORNER)
(R Høibakk, K Storen. 1977).

This variation on the East Ridge goes right of the normal route from the ramp under the Yellow Patch up a yellow diedre (5°) and joins the normal route after three rope lengths.

228. EAST RIDGE DIRECT
(Party unknown)

Almost as popular as the North Ridge of Romsdalshorn. A series of variations on the Original Route adds both character and interest. Easy access, fine situations and good views make it a very popular climb of its grade and justifiably so. 3 hours. 450m, Grade III. Diag pg 117

From the foot of the East Couloir, move immediately right on a rock ramp until it ends below a vertical wall. Ascend the wall by a deep crack, slightly overhanging to finish (4°) to ledges. (This is quite hard and is often avoided by taking a higher ramp from the couloir). Climb up slabby rocks (2°) to the foot of the vertical wall. Move up left and gain a pedestal at the top of the wall by a good ramp (3°). Traverse right on steep rock to a niche and escape through this onto slabs (3°sup). Move left on slabs in a nice position beneath overhangs (3°) to ledges on the left side of the ridge. Continue by three or four pitches up cracks and chimneys (3°) to the summit ridge.

229. NORTH RIDGE
(Party unknown)

Seldom used except in descent. 3 hours. Grade I.

Ascend the hillside from Stigfoss to Bispevatn (The Bishop's Lake) on the west side of Bispen (there is a path by its outlet stream). In the early season it is then possible to walk across the frozen lake without difficulty though later in the year the east shore must be followed over snow and boulders. Either way, it is eventually necessary to scramble up the hillside (often snow) to the col between

Kongen and Bispen (bivouac site in boulders). A cairned path then zig-zags up between small rock walls on the north ridge with only a little scrambling.

230. DESCENT BY THE ORDINARY ROUTE

Easy scrambling to the south west, mostly on scree moving left at halfway, into the lower gully then down the hillside (some glissading usually possible, especially in early season) to the Stigfoss souvenir shops and café.

Many parties prefer to descend by the North Ridge (see below) which has no real difficulties and is well cairned. Either way, about 1–2 hours, the North Ridge taking longest but being the best marked.

231. DESCENT BY THE NORTH RIDGE

Cairns are followed without difficulty to the col or leftwards towards the snow slopes above the lake. Continue along the lake's edge (or on the lake itself if well frozen) to the hillside above Stigfoss and down to the road. About 2 hours.

Immediately north of Bispen is the middle peak of the trio:

Kongen 1,593m (5,225ft)

232. SOUTH WEST FACE, ORDINARY ROUTE
(C Hall, M Soggemoen, E Norahagen. 1882)

This route which passes through impressive mountain scenery ascends by a system of ridges and snow couloirs and presents few obstacles if the easiest line is followed, though there is much snow in the early season. 3 hours from Stigfoss. Grade II inf.

Ascend to the col between Kongen and Bispen by Route 229 and follow Kongen's gently rising southern approach ridge until it abuts against the south wall. (This point may be also reached from Innfjord by a comparatively long approach up the valley of Hangbotn to the saddle under Kongen's West Ridge, then continuing round to the South Ridge.) From here, trend leftwards across occasional ribs and up snow couloirs until almost at the top where it is best to move back right over a ridge and up rock (2°) on the left side of the final couloir. (Bivouac hut to the north west of the summit).

233. SOUTH RIDGE
(Party unknown)

Enjoyable climbing on good rock. 3 hours from Stigfoss. 300m. Grade III.

Follow the Ordinary Route to the foot of the south face. The South Ridge is then followed as directly as possible up the left edge of the wall, to a chimney. Climb this (4°) and move over chockstones at the top to regain the ridge which is then followed to the summit.

234. WEST RIDGE
(Party unknown)

Seldom used except in descent as part of the Kongen ridge system. About 5 hours. Grade II inf.

The usual approach is from Innfjord, up Hangbotn to the saddle between Finnan and Kongen. The west ridge is then followed with some scrambling.

235. SOUTH WALL, GERMAN ROUTE
(D Nagel, W Rein. 1963)

A good route following a natural line up the right side of the wall with some excellent crack pitches in the upper half. About 6 hours. 600m. Grade V inf.

From the col between Kongen and Bispen scramble a little way up the south ridge then contour easily across broken rock to the snow couloir under the South Wall. An obvious ramp of easy rock defines

the lower right side of the wall. It is gained by a pitch on steep rock (5°) and followed easily up right for four pitches until beneath corners trending left. Gain the corners by two pitches (3°, 5°inf) and continue more easily (1°,2°) until it steepens again. Three pitches (4°, 3°, 5°inf) bring one to easier rock which is crossed right, then left to the Terrace beneath the Flake Crack. Ascend this for 60m (5°sup, 6°, 5°sup) to the ridge which is followed for a rope length past a large pinnacle (4°). Easy scrambling follows to the top.

236. SOUTH WALL, VARIATION
(Party unknown)

Less climbing is involved than on the German Route but it is of comparable standard and easier access. About 5 hours. 360m. Grade V inf.

Follow Route 232 to the South Wall, and descend 18m right to the start of the climb Ascend a ramp leading right then left for 15m (4°) to reach an obvious rightwards

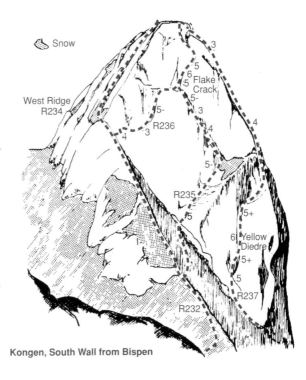

Kongen, South Wall from Bispen

traverse. Move along this for 120m (3°) to the foot of a corner crack. Climb this for 60m (5°inf) to The Terrace and move right along this for a rope length past a large pinnacle, to the base of the Flake Crack. The German Route is then followed to the summit.

The next routes start down in the depths of Isterdal:

237. SOUTH EAST FACE
(A Howard, B Tweedale, R Holt, W Gartside. 1967)

A long, varied, and interesting route, though with some vegetation on the lower slabs and a little loose rock on the South East Wall. Completely free throughout, no more than six pegs being used on any pitch. The first ascent took 3¹/₂ days, the party having a mass of food and equipment for tackling the 21m roof on the Direct which was then unclimbed. They were forced to retreat from this by waterfalls of snow melt, having attempted the climb too early in the season.

The best bivouac place with snow and water is in the great scree basin beneath the South East Wall. It is possible to escape from here without difficulty to the saddle under the south ridge, thereby reducing the seriousness of the route. It may be possible to complete the ascent in one day if the lower 600m is climbed by much easier pitches to the left. If the route is followed throughout, most parties will require 1¹/₂ days. About 1,800m. Grade V sup. Photos and diags pgs 119, 121, 122 and right.

Approach from the road in Isterdal via Kløvstien (Route 220) which has bridges

across the river, then toil up through the trees to the bottom of the face. In the centre of the slab base, a huge overlap curves over to the left. 90m or so left of the bottom of this is a groove going straight up the slabs. The start is usually across snow then 90m up the groove (4°) to ledges. Easily left for a pitch and then straight up delicate slabs (5°sup) to the upper left end of the huge overlap. A further pitch (3°) leads up to the great diagonal rake which slants easily up right to the central snow patch. From here, move out left to beneath overhangs (3°) then a pitch first left and then back right between overlaps (6° pegs) on steep greasy rock. Continue trending right through overlapping slabs for another rope length (5°), then five pitches (4°) first by a wide chimney on the left, then a wet crack and chimney to the right and finally up slabs

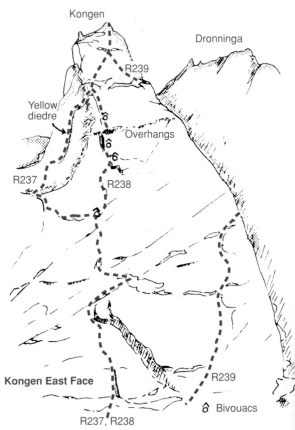

Kongen

Dronninga

R239

Yellow diedre

Overhangs

R237

R238

Kongen East Face

R239

ô Bivouacs

R237, R238

R237

and scree to a large ledge left of the South East Wall. Good bivouac site with water.

A horizontal line can now be seen just above, leading out across the wall to the long open Yellow Diedre in its centre. From the ledge, move up a slab and make a hard move (6°inf) to gain a stance on blocks at the start of the traverse. Follow this rightwards for two pitches (5°) rising up on good holds, but sometimes loose and finishing by a diagonal tension traverse down right to better ledges. Follow these easily for another pitch to the overhanging chimney marking the start of the Yellow Diedre. Climb a good pitch (5°sup) up a hidden groove left of the chimney and then rightwards above it in an exposed position into the open diedre. A serious pitch now follows for 45m (6° pegs), very steep, with some loose rock and final overhanging chimney. Escape through this by an airy pitch (5°) to a vast ledge under the South East Ridge. Cross the ledge to the far back wall and slant left up a slab, then go straight up by a steep

trending left to a terrace with snow and water. The right end of the ledge is directly below the 21m overhang of the East Face Direct. Bivouac site.

From the left end of the terrace, a slab goes easily to the top of an open gully then a short corner and leftwards traverse (5°) lead to an overhanging black chimney. Avoid this by a hidden groove on its right and a difficult move left to its top (6°, pegs). (If dry, it may be easier to take the chimney direct.) Easy scrambling now follows for about 240m first left to a stream then back right across slabs

crack (5°) and finally an easy chimney onto the ridge and the upper east face. Bivouac site; snow.

Easy scrambling up the east face near the snowfield is followed by a rope length up a gully (3°). Three pitches (3°, 3°sup) of grooved slabs trending right lead to a traverse beneath a steep wall. A further three pitches zig-zagging through bulges (3°, 3°) bring one to the final expanse of slabs. These can be taken at almost any point (2°, 3°), the original route trending right to beneath the summit tower which was climbed by its right arête.

238. EAST FACE DIRECT
(B Thompson, J Teigland,
J Stanger, D Walsh. 1967)

A superb route taking a
direct line up the east face.
Starting by easy angled
slabs, the route gradually
steepens to the crux of the
climb 'The 21m roof' which
involves over 33m of artifi-
cial climbing and a stance in
etriers at the end of it.
Water is available on most
of the climb except near the
roof. A retreat from below
the roof would be difficult.
Once above, it is best to
continue upwards even in
bad conditions as retreat is
then almost impossible.

It should be stressed that
rainfall or, in the early
season, melting snow, can
transform the face beneath
the roof from 'snuff dry
slabs' to a waterfall in less
than an hour (see
comments in Route 237). It
is possible a fast party could
reach the Fourth Bivouac or the better
ledges above from the Second Bivouac in one
day, thus obviating the need for hammocks
at the Third as there are no good bivouac
sites between these points.

Every type of peg was used on the first
ascent from knife blades to large bongs; very
few were left in place. Five bolts were fixed
in the roof. 4¹/₂ days. 1,360m. Grade VI sup.
Photo and diag pg 120 and 122.

Approach and climb directly up to the first
bivouac by the South East Face Route (Route
237) with pitches of 5° and 6° pegs, or take
the easier line to the left, as on the first
ascent of the Direct; this is mainly 2°, 3°
until a band of steeper slabs is reached.
These are crossed in two rope lengths from
right to left (5°, 4°) and then give way to
easier ground leading to grassy terraces
below the steep wall. The bivouac site is at
the highest point that can be reached
without difficulty.

From the bivouac, traverse right to a steep
wall which is climbed for 15m to a good
ledge (4°). Move left, and up an overhanging
crack (5°, wedge) then up a rake slanting left
to a ledge below a black wall. (This is below
and left of the two prominent overhangs
below the main roof). Here there are two
possible lines the most obvious being the
Norwegian Variant from a previous attempt.
This follows a wide crack in the corner
between the black wall and the overhangs
(bongs). Alternatively, as on the first ascent,
follow a line of thin cracks for 60m (A1, A2)
with many knife-blades, and stances in
etriers, passing over small overhangs to a line
of bigger ones.

Descend a few feet then traverse the steep
wall on the right (6°) to gain the upper part

of the crack ascended by the Norwegian Variant. Follow this (4°) to the overhangs then climb the wall on the right (5°) to good ledges on a great sweep of slabs above roofs. Second Bivouac.

Climb the slabs to the cracks leading to the big black roof. Traverse left, then straight up a steep crack for 30m (6° very loose). Continue more easily up the crack until it steepens; belay. Here, a traverse right was made for 6m (5°, 3 pegs) into a bottomless corner where hammocks were slung for the Third Bivouac.

Continue up the crack (A2, bongs) until it is possible to traverse onto the black wall below the roof (5°, very loose). Belay on a very narrow ledge on the wall. Climb the crack on the right side of the wall (A2, bongs) to a small overhang (bolt in place above). Continue to the main roof (A2) then follow the crack between the roof and the wall (A3, wedges, bongs, threads and 3 bolts) to the edge of the roof. Climb a wide, rotten chimney for a few metres (A4) until a traverse left can be made (A3). Continue up the wall above the roof (knife blades and 2 bolts) to a good crack where a stance can be made in etriers. From the belay on the wall to the stance over the roof – 33m (8 hours). Traverse left for 12m (5°, A1) to a small ledge. Fourth Bivouac (bolt in place).

Continue traversing up to the left across a steep slab (6°, 1 bolt, 1 peg) then up easier cracks for 36m (5°, A1) to a short wall. Climb this (5°) to a good terrace. Descend an easy chimney to reach very good ledges to the right (bivouac sites). Climb a beautiful wide chimney for 90m (4°, 5°) until the angle eases, and much easier ground (3°, 2°) as for the South East Face Route, leads to the summit.

239. EAST FACE, ORIGINAL ROUTE
(A R Heen, T Krohn, S N Meyer. 1939)

The route – a big route for its day – begins on slabs at the bottom right of the East Face and avoids the steep section by the couloir on its right. The couloir can be difficult after wet weather. 7–9 hours. About 1,800m. Grade IV sup. Diag pg 120.

Cross the river by the lower Kløvstien bridge (Route 220) then up through the birch woods to reach the climb. Ascend diagonally right by grass patches and easy slabs from the bottom centre of the face until a large smooth slab is reached. This is ascended by a thin crack (4°). Continue diagonally right to a large crescent-shaped corner formed by a flake projecting from the face. Climb the corner (5°) and continue in the same line until a grass ledge is reached below steep slabs (cairn). Two ways are now possible. The Original trends right into the great couloir between Kongen and Dronninga (about three pitches) which is followed to a subsidiary couloir in the north face.

The Direct Variant continues straight up slabs for a rope length with increasing difficulty to a peg belay and sling stance in a grassy groove (6°). Traverse right for 15m then rapidly up another grass-filled groove (6°) and belay well back. Up the corner slightly left in two pitches (5°) with a peg for protection on the awkwardly bulging exit to the terrace. This is followed easily rightwards to the great couloir between Kongen and Dronninga. (From this point, the irregular patch of rock on Dronninga's south wall resembles the face of a troll.)

The 300m subsidiary gully in the left wall of the couloir then gives straightforward climbing to snow ledges above the steep east wall. Two traverses (6°) may be necessary to avoid waterfalls at $\frac{1}{3}$ and $\frac{3}{4}$ height whilst the last section is climbed by its left wall and the easy-angled ridge to the boulder strewn ledges. Steep grooves and corners are now climbed, slightly right of centre (4°) then, as the angle eases, trend left by a short steep wall to the summit.

240. DESCENT BY THE ORDINARY ROUTE

Start west of the south ridge, by a cairned gully and bear right as soon as possible into a parallel snow couloir. Continue the descent, trending left to gain the south ridge. Do NOT go straight down the gullies as they mostly end in steep slabs. The route is then by the shores of the Bishop's Lake, and down to Stigfoss. About 2 hours.

Dronninga 1,568m (5,143ft)

241. WEST RIDGE, ORDINARY ROUTE
(C Hall, M Soggemoen, E Norahagen. 1882)

There are few difficulties. The route is rarely used except in descent. 4 hours from Stigfoss. Grade II inf.

Follow Route 229 to the head of Bispevatn and so northwards up the hillside (snow) to the saddle beneath Kongen's west ridge (or approach here from Innfjord, via Hangbotn). Continue north, bypassing Prinsessa Pinnacle and follow scree gullies to the ridge. Once on the summit, the highest pinnacle is the one nearest Kongen.

242. NORTH RIDGE
(B Helseth, A Rypdal. 1928)

A route seldom used nowadays but probably the easiest way to the summit. 5 hours from Isterdal seter. Grade I.

From Isterdal seter, follow the track up to the low col of Urkleiva, 3km north of Dronninga. Follow the broad vegetated shoulder of the ridge, over Karitind and up to the pinnacled top of Dronninga.

243. EAST FACE
(R and S N Meyer. 1939. Direct Start as described below: A R Heen, O Lundh, S N Meyer. 1941)

A good route though the difficulties could be greater after wet weather as the route follows a gully cutting through steep slabs. 14 hours. About 1,500m. Grade IV sup.

Scramble to the top of the birch slopes which protrude high onto the east face, and climb cracked slabs to a short open gully with a steep crag on the left. Climb up to the left for 18m and then up a narrow but distinct ledge and long slabs to a spacious terrace with a large holed block. Move up to the broad cavity left of the block then bear right to another terrace which leads across to a steep distinct gully which affords the easiest way through steep rocks above. Follow this narrow gully, often with torrents,

to a hollow below a large projecting rock. Trend left across slabs to a point above the first pinnacle on the East Ridge which is then followed to the top.

244. EAST RIDGE
(A R Heen, B Botolfsen, A Heyerdahl. 1941)

A good route on quite steep rock following the left side of the east face and finishing up the well-defined east ridge. 15 hours. About 1,500m. Grade V.

From the top of the birch slope below the east face, bear left towards the main couloir between Dronninga and Kongen, then fork right up a large open gully. Move sharply left across a difficult gully which terminates below a large narrow gully cave. Move up on the overhang and through a chimney to a grassy slope. Snow and water. (It is possible to escape right from here onto the East Face Route.)

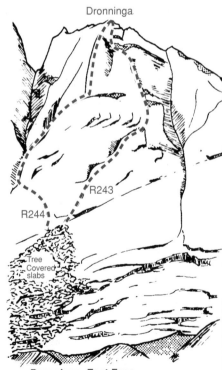

Dronninga, East Face

Move up the large plateau and follow the right side of the ridge by increasingly steep and exposed climbing eventually bearing left to a pinnacle on the ridge where the angle eases and the summit is gained by easier climbing.

245. DESCENT BY THE ORDINARY ROUTE

Descend scree gullies leftwards to the saddle under Kongen, then down by Bispevatn to Stigfoss. 3 hours.

246. DESCENT BY THE NORTH RIDGE

The broad ridge is followed over Karitind to the saddle and tarn of Urkleiva, and so down into Isterdal. About 3 hours.

Prinsessa Pinnacle

247. NORTH AND SOUTH SIDES
(A R Heen, M Borg. 1946)

This is the westernmost pinnacle on the west ridge. It can be climbed without difficulty from north or south, and the ascent may be combined with any nearby route. Grade I

Karitind 1,439m (4,721ft)

248. BY THE NORTH RIDGE
(C Hall, M Soggemoen, E Norahagen.1882)

This peak is rarely visited but is easy of access and has good views. About 3–4 hours. Grade I.

Approach easily from Isterdal seter by Route 242, which crosses Karitind on its way to Dronninga 1.5km further the south.

The ridge north of Urkleiva (the pass through which Route 221 goes) has six tops but only the most northerly is ascended regularly and has good views of Åndalsnes, the valleys and the fjord.

Setnesfjell 1,190m (3,903ft)

This is the last, most northerly top, above the village of Veblungsnes.

249. SOUTH EAST FACE, ORDINARY ROUTE
(B Campbell-Kelly and A Ferguson. 1970).

This is the obvious rock bowl high on the right-hand side of the entrance to Isterdal valley. Access is along a side road marked 'Hankamhaug 0.5'. Ease of access and the relatively non-serious situation make this a pleasant one day climb. Water is available at the base of the main cliff. The main feature of the cliff is a huge curving overhang. This is at the top of a vast scoop of smooth rock about 150m high. At the base of the cliff is a black leftward slanting gashed groove. 8 hours. Approx 1,000m Grade V.

Climb up the stream-bed for 350m (4° in places) keeping to the left where it steepens near the top. The route takes a line almost directly up from here. It avoids the scoop and the overhang by climbing the rock just to the right of these.

From the stream move left to the gashed groove. Climb the left side of the groove (3°) for 60m until it closes, then move right onto slabs and climb these (4°) to a good stance. Left for 3m, and continue up the slabs (4°sup) to belay in a huge groove, 40m. Carry on to the left over more slabs (piton at 10m), a leftward rising traverse (5°sup) for 15m brings one to a poor stance at the base of a leftward slanting groove. Follow the groove for 45m (5°sup), a fine sustained pitch. Easier climbing for 45m leads to a large terrace at the bottom of the big scoop. Walk along the terrace for 45m to its right end and belay at the base of a steep vege-tated chimney. Climb the chimney and gain the arête at the top with difficulty (5°sup) 45m. Climb the slabs above moving right into a groove after 45m (5°). Follow the groove (4°, loose) to a grassy bay with good belays on the right. Cross the bay and gain the arête on the left by a short overhanging crack (4°sup). Follow the arête for 10m, and belay. Move up and left for 15m to a corner containing loose blocks, traverse right for 4m with difficulty then up and back left (15m) to belay in a black corner at the back of a grassy ledge. (5°sup). Climb up and left across two steep grooves (5° with one sling for aid) and belay at the back of a large grass bay. From the left end of the bay move right up slabs, (3°). Good belay. Two pitches of steep scrambling lead to the ridge and thence the summit.

250. DESCENT

Via the North East Ridge to Veblungsnes. 2¹/₂ hours.

Or, walk down the ridge in a south easterly direction, following the top of the amphitheatre. Go past a steep loose chimney and the overhanging wall to where it is possible to abseil easily back into the amphitheatre. Four abseils take one to terraces and patches of trees leading to the top of the stream. Descend through the trees on the south side of the stream. 2 hours to the road.

251. SOUTH EAST FACE DIRECT
(B Campbell-Kelly and A Ferguson. 1970)

This climbs the large smooth scoop in the centre of the cliff, moves left under the huge overhang and climbs the steep wall just to the left. Sustained and difficult free climbing with some fine positions. Four points of aid used. 11 hours. Approx 1,000m. Grade VI.

Follow the South East Face Route to the end of the terrace beneath the vegetated chimney at the base of the scoop. Belay. Climb the groove above and follow the flake crack for

20m until it steepens again (5°sup). Climb the steep groove with difficulty moving left onto the arête after 8m (6°sup), follow the flakes up for 15m to a good belay. Follow the obvious rising traverse line leftwards for 25m and make difficult moves for 5m to belay at the base of the obvious wide crack containing a loose chockstone (5°sup).

Climb the crack (6°) and follow a traverse line left to a thin crack, climb this with difficulty (6°sup) and move left to belay on the right of a smooth slabby scoop (45m). Step left onto the slab and climb up for 3m to place a peg in the corner beneath a small overlap. Use tension from this to gain a bottomless groove on the left. Climb this and cross slabs to a short corner. Climb the corner (2m) and move left to a fine stance and good belays (30m 6°sup). Step round the arête and climb the wall for 20m (5°), move right onto a large ledge on the arête. Arrange protection and move back left onto the wall. Using a good flake and concealed holds move up into a strenuous position and place a blade piton in a vertical overlap (difficult, piton removed). Use a long sling on this to make a difficult move left to gain a better ledge with a loose pinnacle (6°sup.). Move right and up more easily for 5m to the bottom of a short overhanging wall. Climb this with 2 pegs for aid and belay on a good ledge (45m, 6°sup). Traverse left for 6m, climb the pleasant steep wall and follow easy

View from Kongen to Stighorn (centre) and Bispen (right)

slabs trending right (45m, 4°). Climb loose slabs on the right to gain a grassy bay (45m, 3°). Two pitches of scrambling leftwards lead to the ridge.

Descent As for the previous route.

252. EAST FACE
(H C Due and party. 1872)

A long scramble up gullies and scree. 2–3 hours. Grade I.

Follow the gully of Setnesgrova to the top of a shoulder – Store Nuken. (Impressive rock scenery in the gully and some scrambling.) The summit is gained by easy scrambling up the East Face.

253. NORTH EAST RIDGE
(C Hall, M Soggemoen. 1899)

The ridge is considerably forested in its lower half and has steep grassy scrambling above. About 2–3 hours. Grade I.

Cross fields behind the village of Veblungsnes and follow a narrow winding track up through birch trees to the top of the shoulder of Lille Nuken. The path now fades and the scrambling becomes steeper to the summit with detours to avoid bulges on the ridge.

Solo winter ascent by A Howard in 1967. Excellent conditions suitable for crampons right from the house door in Veblungsnes!

254. NORTH WEST RIDGE
(A Howard, B Tweedale. Winter 1967)

Follows the ridge in its entirety as seen from Åndalsnes. Mostly scrambling in good scenery. About 4 hours. Grade III inf.

After the second tunnel on the old Ålesund coast road scramble up the hillside keeping left of the Insteelva stream which flows out of the high corrie south of Setnesfjell. Keep left onto the shoulder below the first cliff and, to avoid the only real difficulty, pass it on its right by grassy scrambling. Or, harder, take the Direct Variant, ascend grassy slabs for a rope length (4°) then a steep corner left

of the arête for a second pitch (5°sup, 2 pegs).

Further scrambling up the ridge leads to the upper cliff which is about 180m and is climbed by zig-zags mainly on the right side (3°). The ridge beyond here becomes progressively narrower and is quite sharp just below the top (2°).

255. DESCENT BY THE NORTH EAST RIDGE

This is the usual route of descent, zig-zagging steeply down into Veblungsnes. 1 hour.

Around the base of Setnesfjell are three overhanging cliffs, all 60–90m high and giving good practice in artificial climbing on a rainy day. The first is halfway up the east side of the shoulder of Lille Nuken, and is Blåmann's Cliff and Cave. The cave entrance, which is very small, is beneath the crag and opens into a chamber about 15m high and 60m long. The other two cliffs are above the eastern ends of the first two tunnels on the old Ålesund road.

256. THE BISPEN, KONGEN AND DRONNINGA RIDGE

A well worthwhile mountain tour with a good choice of routes to suit most parties up to Grade V if the South Wall climb of Kongen is included. From and to Stigfoss, 10 hours. Grade II inf.

Ascend to the summit of Bispen by the South Ridge (II inf) or, perhaps, by the East Ridge. Descend by the North Ridge (I) to the saddle, and up by the South West Face (II inf) or the South Ridge (III) to the top of Kongen. Descend Kongen by the West Ridge (II inf) to the saddle and up to the top of Dronninga by its West Ridge (II inf).

Return to Stigfoss by Route 245, or alternatively continue the ridge down to Urkleiva and Isterdal seter via the summit of Karitind (Route 246). From Urkleiva (a pleasant bivouac site with wood and water) it is of course possible to continue northward over the remaining six summits and down into Veblungsnes by the North East Ridge of Setnesfjell.

The Finnan Group

Finnan and its glaciers, behind Bispen and Kongen, seen from the walk to Store Trolltind

This group of peaks which are high summits of an alpine nature yet with easy access are, despite being in the central area, seldom climbed. Finnan, which is the second highest peak in the central massif, presents a complex system of ridges and pinnacles to the west and has a fairly large glacier to the east ending in an ice fall above the Bishop's Lake. Further west of Finnan is the peak of Middagstind, then to the south the massif ends at the pass on the Innfjord–Trollstig Pass walk.

For climbers visiting the Finnan Group, there is accommodation in Romsdal, Isterdal and also at Innfjord. Up in the hills, there is a boulder bivouac in the entrance to the hanging valley of Smørbotn. It is situated just above the tree-line beneath boulder slopes on the south west shoulder of Middagsfjell. Few routes have been made in this group and the descriptions to existing climbs are mostly vague. With future exploration there is no doubt that numerous good new routes will be discovered.

All the eastern corries facing the Åndalsnes–Valldal road hold glaciers and permanent snowfields, though they are shrinking fast. Westwards the valleys are lower and more pastoral. Access to the eastern side is from the Stigfoss cafés. It is on these slopes near the pass that the ski championships are held, snow permitting, in early June, the road being opened for the end of May.

From the west the usual start is the village of Innfjord about 16km by road from Åndalsnes along the shores of Romsdalsfjord towards Ålesund. The western side of the group is defined by the valley of Innfjord up which there is a road for 8km to Berill. From here, there are tracks and walks going east and south east over the mountains beyond the Romsdal area (see Route 274).

There is a also a good walk which defines the southern limit of this massif and goes over the mountain pass east of Berill, reaching the Valldal road about 2km south of the Trollstig Pass and 7km from the cafés at the top of the Stigfoss waterfall:

257. WALK FROM INNFJORD TO THE TROLLSTIG PASS

This pleasant walk can be done as a precursor to, or continuation of, the Langfjelldal to Vermedal Walk (Route 138). 12km.

From Berill, head south then east up Berdalen for about 6km to reach the pass of Småhola at 1,088m. Contour south past three small lakes then descend increasingly steeply to reach the Valldal road about 2km south of the Trollstig Pass and opposite the start of the Langfjelldal to Verma walk.

The main peak of the area is:

Finnan 1,800m (5,904ft)

258. SOUTH EAST RIDGE
(C Hall, M Soggemoen, E Norahagen. 1898)

The easiest and most accessible route to the summit. 3 hours from Stigfoss. Grade II inf.

From the Stigfoss huts, scramble up the side of the stream, almost to the Bispevatn, and then onto the shoulder and ridge which passes over two minor tops (Østre and Midtre Finnan) and then ascends nicely angled snow to the summit of Søndre Finnan, possibly corniced. The South East Ridge (snow) is then followed to the highest summit with the eastern glacier beneath.

The peak has also been climbed from Innfjord, probably via Småhola or Smørbotn, but the route is not known.

259. DESCENT BY THE ORDINARY ROUTE

Down the South East Ridge to Stigfoss. 2 hours.

260. FINNAN NORTH EAST GLACIER
(K Svanemyr, A Gruner, B Østigard, H Doseth. 1976).

From Bispevatnet (reached from Stigfoss via the Bispen approach) ascend the glacier, some ice to start, then the centre of the wall of Finnan. Grade II.

Søndre Finnan

261. EAST RIDGE
(C Hall, M Soggemoen, E Norahagen. 1898)

This is part of Route 258 to the main summit of Finnan. About 2 hours. Grade I.

262. SOUTH EAST FACE
(F Davies, T Lee. 1967)

An enjoyable mountaineering route. About 3–4 hours for the round trip. Grade III.

From the road, scramble up the hillside and cross the south east glacier until below the highest part of the South East Face. This is climbed for 180m by the easiest line to the summit ridge.

263. DESCENT BY THE ORDINARY ROUTE

Easily down the East Ridge (some snow) and hillside to Stigfoss. 1 hour.

Midtre Finnan

Viewed from the Trollstig Pass this is the left-hand of two prominent rock spurs rising from the south east glacier to the east ridge of Søndre Finnan.

264. SOUTH RIDGE
(K Chadwick, A Howard. 1968)

A pleasant little climb in good alpine surroundings. 1–1½ hours. 120m. Grade III.

From Stigfoss or the Trollstig Pass walk up onto Finnan's South East Glacier and cross this to below the pinnacles. Start below the centre of the left top beneath a fairly obvious slanting chimney. Don't climb the chimney but climb for 60m (3°sup) by winding shallow grooves trending left then right to below the yellow wall. Climb about 4m up a cracked leaning corner (4°inf) and move right to below a prominent yellow diedre. (This has been climbed to the roofs (6°inf) but pegs will be required above.) Avoid the diedre by a 45m rightward traverse on a ramp (2°) to the East Ridge and up this for 15m to the top.

Østre Finnan

To the right of Midtre Finnan.

265. SOUTH RIDGE
(A Howard, K Chadwick. 1968)

*Similar to its left-hand partner. 120m.
Grade III.*

Approach as for the previous route and start
about 6m right of the ridge leading to the
right-hand top. Follow a shallow groove up
right, then move right at its top and ascend a
steep wall on good holds (3°sup) to a ledge.
Above, take the left of two corners (3°sup) to
its end then follow the right corner till it
leads onto the ridge which is climbed for
60m (2°, 3°inf) to a yellow wall. Climb this
by steep cracks (3°) and trend right to finish
at the cairn.

North west of Berill and about 4km almost
directly south of Innfjorden as the crow flies
are Middagsfjell and Middagstind,
approached by the track into the hanging
valley of Smørbotn. The start of the path is
not obvious. Follow the Innfjord–Berill road
to a point 300m beyond the bridge over the
Smørbotn stream which is just over 1km
south of Innfjord. Now, take the left fork, and
continue past a gate beyond which the lane
curves right. 20m before a red hut, a track
goes left into the pine trees. Follow this into
the woods (avoiding the first turn on the
right). After a couple of bends it goes almost
directly up the hillside into Smørbotn. (About
1½ hours from Innfjord).

Summit view, Finnan area

Middagsfjell

266. NORTH EAST RIDGE
(Climbers from Molde)

There are good views from here but the mountain is rarely visited except as an approach to the peak of Middagstind. 3 hours from Innfjord. Grade I.

Scrambling up boulder slopes (at the foot of which is a bivouac) brings one to the North East Ridge. This is then followed to the main top without difficulty. It then becomes progressively narrower with numerous small pinnacles – some climbing (2°) and abseiling necessary if taken direct, until the gap is reached below Middagstind.

267. DESCENT BY THE EAST SIDE

This presents no difficulty. ½ hour to the bivouac, then ½ hour to Innfjord.

Middagstind 1,556m (5,104ft)

268. NORTH EAST RIDGE
(Climbers from Molde)

The dominant summit south of Innfjord, hence 'Midday Mountain'. Seen from the hanging valley of Smørbotn it has a beautifully slender church-spire summit. The rock is mossy but this is compensated for by the excellent situations on the summit tower. 6 hours from Innfjord. 420m Grade IV sup.

Approach via Route 266 to the gap below the steep ridge and follow the grassy ramp and boulders up right to a little col. Descend the other side and move across grassy ledges to a chimney and the start of the climb proper. Up to a ledge, then left by slabs and up a steep cracked wall past a peg (5°sup). Continue upwards avoiding difficulties by bearing right, then left until a platform is reached on the ridge (3°).

Follow the narrow crest of the ridge, and a difficult leaning groove (5°) to a traverse right, then go back up left to ledges. Steep, good cracks up the buttress (4°) lead to easy ground on the ridge ahead and the next rope

length is barred only by an awkward crack (5°). Above, the ridge steepens again and becomes increasingly narrow. Continue, first by a hidden chimney on the left (4°) then up the crest and a hanging groove (5°) on the right. Flakes and cracks are now followed up the left wall (4°), sometimes with arms spanning both sides of the ridge to the final summit crack (4°).

The main top is actually beyond this point but no description is available at present. It is necessary to cross pinnacles and a gap to the final ridge.

269. DESCENT BY THE NORTH EAST RIDGE

It is possible to climb down the ridge to the traverse line above the leaning groove. From here an abseil can be made to ledges above the initial chimney, and Route 267 followed from the gap. 3–4 hours to Innfjord.

It is, presumably, also possible (and probably easier) to descend south eastwards into Berdal and then by road back to Innfjord. Nothing is known of this route.

The Western Ranges

Taskedalstind, between Valldal and Berill

This is the large area of lesser-known mountains between Romsdalsfjord and Valldal, south west of the pass from Innfjord to the Trollstig road. Few modern routes have been made in these ranges, except on Blåstolen and perhaps the Trollvasstind–Middagstind group. All that is given here, therefore, is a brief resume of the known first ascents, together with information on a few walks. (*Fra Topp til Topp i Romsdal* describes many good scrambles and winter tours in this area.)

Ringshorn 1,532m (5,056ft)

This is the peak immediately south of the Innfjord to Trollstig Pass walk (Route 257) and just above the Trollstig road.

270. BY THE NORTH WEST RIDGE
(Party unknown)

An easy scramble, mostly snow, often used by skiers. About 2 hours, Grade I.

From just south of the Trollstig Pass, where the walks to Innerdal and Verma start, cross the river and scramble up the hillside to the snow slopes under the north face. (Possible avalanche danger from cornices in the very early season.) Continue upwards to the saddle below the ridge, which is followed to the top.

271. EAST RIDGE
(Party unknown)

A rocky scramble starting near the above route. About 1 hour. Grade I.

Ascend the hillside to reach easy scrambling up slabs which steepen a little, below the summit, with a short steep wall to the left.

Descent by the same route. About ½ hour.

Storfjell 1,560m (5,117ft)

This peak is a couple of kilometres west of Ringshorn.

272. BY THE NORTH WEST FACE
(C Hall, M Soggemoen. 1900)

Reached easily from the pass on the Berill path. Grade I

Hesten and Lille Hesten
1,556m (5,104ft)

273.
(C Hall, M Soggemoen. 1900)

These peaks are south west of the Trollstig–Berill path (Route 257). They can be traversed in one day from and to Berill, with some rock scrambling if desired. Grade I or II dependent on choice of route.

Access to the peaks further south such as Ådalstind (1,433m) Taskedalstind (1,609m) and Grønnfonntind (1,657m) is usually from Valldal or the Trollstig road between Valldal and Åndalsnes. A good trail with huts bisects the area.

274. WALK FROM VALLDAL TO BERILL

There is a mountain path from Valldal to Berill or Pusken seter (the Fokkhaug tourist hut) which is situated in the centre of these ranges. The path starts at Myklebust seter just north of Valldal on the E63 (about 7km north east of the fjord) and goes northwards over a pass at 900m, between Taskedalstind and Ådalstind, to join the path from Innfjord. It is a 6 hour journey (approximately 24km) passing the hut of Fattig og Rik at about15km. This could be linked with the Innerdal to Trollstig walk (Route 257) back to the Trollstig Pass, meeting the E63 25km up from the starting point.

Alternatively, from the hut of Fattig og Rik, there is a choice of walks to the west for about 9km to the hut of Fokhaugstova at Pusken seter, then on to Stordal or Øvstedal.

Grønnfonntind 1,657m (5,468ft)

275.
(C Hall, M Soggemoen. 1900)

This is the peak 6km east of the pass on the Valldal–Pusken path. Grade I.

Taskedalstind 1,609m (5,310ft)

276.

These peaks just 1km east of the pass were ascended at the same time as the previous summit, first by the middle top and then traversing the whole ridge. The complete circuit, from and to Berill, is reputedly a superb day out. Grade II inf.

277.

Its narrow north ridge can also be climbed. 400m. Grade V.

Seterfjell 1516m, 4972ft

278.
(C Hall, M Soggemoen. 1900)

This is thought to be the ridge between the two above mentioned summits. Grade II inf.

The north western peaks of these ranges are around Måndal where Voll is located on the Åndalsnes–Ålesund road. They are accessible both from the Innfjord–Pusken seter track to their south (Route 274) and from Voll in the north.

279. WALKS FROM BERILL TO MÅNDAL

There is a difficult track from Bøstol on the walk between Fattig og Rik and Berill, which goes over Bryne Skar between Måsvasstind and Nonstind then down to Skaret farm in Volldal, about 7km from Voll. There is also an easier path starting and finishing in the same valleys, but crossing the mountains further east, between Nonstind and Middagstind by the pass at the lake of Tindevatn. As always, campsites are numerous.

Trollvasstind 1,422m (4,693ft)

280.
(C Hall, M Soggemoen. 1897)

*Twin peaks north east of Pusken seter.
Grade I.*

281.
(O Nesje. 1959)

The north face (details not available).

Måsvasstind 1,253m (4,135ft)

282.
(F Jacobsen and L Skare. 1875)

*A long ridge in magnificent surroundings to
the east of the above peak. Grade I.*

Nonstind 1,572m (5,188ft)

283. FROM MÅSVASSTIND
(C Hall, M Soggemoen. 1897)

*This is the next summit to the east, cairned in
1875 by Jacobsen and Skare. The traverse of
the two peaks. Grade I.*

Middagstind 1,569m (5,178ft)

Not to be confused with Middagstind south
of Innfjord!

284.
(J E Furor and the Vold bros. 1895)

This peak rises north west of Berill. Grade I.

285. THE NORTH RIDGE
(Hall, Soggemoen and Skare. 1897)

*The almost vertical rock tower on its north
ridge is called Middagshorn. The ridge is
very narrow and provides good sport.
Grade II inf.*

The first ascent of all the Middagstind
pinnacles was made in 1938 by E Andall, E
Birkeland, E H Falkenthal and T Lundtvedt.

About 4km north of Måndal, overlooking the
road to Ålesund, are the peaks of Trollstolen
and Blåstolen, the latter with its imposing
north face.

Trollstolen 1,330m (4,372ft)

286.
(F Jacobsen and party. 1872)

*This is the most northerly of a little group of
peaks between Voll and Vågstranda on the
Ålesund road. (About 1 hour by bus from
Åndalsnes.) Grade I.*

Blåstolen 1,050m (3,444ft)

The summit was first ascended at the same
time as its neighbour Trollstolen in 1872. It
has a tremendously impressive North Wall
rising sheer from a corrie just above the road
and visible in profile from Åndalsnes 16km
up the fjord to the east. An unsuccessful
attempt was made on it in 1967 following
cracks just right of centre (lower third very
loose). The original route on this wall attacks
by a buttress on the left.

287. NORTH WALL
(C Nielsen and party. 1964)

*From the road the whole route is visible, first
up the obvious tree-covered buttress which
goes up the lower half, then as directly as
possible up the steep wall above to the north
summit.About 11 hours. 450m. VI inf.*

Scramble up into the corrie from the road
and continue by grassy scrambling up the
left-hand side of the tree-covered buttress
until it abuts against the wall. Go rightwards
along a grass shelf to the start of the climb
proper at a point about 30m left of the far
end (cairn).

Trend left on steep rock for two rope lengths
(4°, 5°, 1 peg) and continue a little further in
this line before traversing rightwards over
difficult slabs (6°). Move left again, and keep
left over two small overhangs (5°sup, 1 peg)
to easier climbing straight up towards a grass
ledge (5°). Follow a grass ramp rightwards
(6°, poor pegs, difficult and dangerous), then

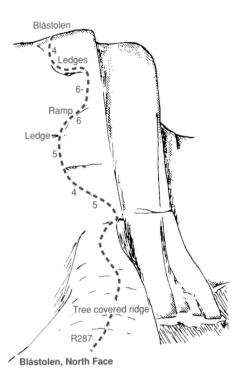

Blåstolen, North Face

trend up right by steep but good climbing for
two pitches (6°inf, 1 peg, 6°inf), to a large
terrace. From the left end of this climb first
steeply (4°), then more easily (3°sup) to the
top.

Another route was added in 1987 (see
Klatring i Romsdal).

288. DESCENT BY THE NORTH EAST RIDGE

After initial steep rocks the angle eases
becoming more vegetated until the road is
reached.1 hour.

The Southern Ranges and Dovrefjell

Approaching Snøhetta's summit in winter

These mountains which are in the Tafjord and Dovre areas to the south and south east of Romsdal, include some of the most remote peaks in and around Romsdal and also the highest. For the climber, the Tafjord peaks have little to offer being mostly rounded snow summits, though some climbs have been done on Snøhetta in the Dovre mountains further east. The whole district is well served by marked trails and tourist huts, two of those in the Tafjord area – Reindalseter and Kaldhusseter – being 'full-service' courtesy of the Sunnmøre Touring Association (ÅST). The whole region consequently provides ample opportunities for good walking tours, many described in *Walking in Norway* (Cicerone Press) and *Norway South, Valley and Mountain Walks* (Rother).

The Southern Ranges

Access to these mountains from the west is by ferry or road from Valldal up to the village of Tafjord at the head of Nordalsfjord. From here there is a road to Røddal from which it is necessary to walk up to Reindal seter (tourist hut). The highest summits are east of here. The approach from the east is from Bjorli, which is north of Dombås, before the road descends dramatically into Romsdal. There is a choice of accommodation in Bjorli including the Saga Inn tourist centre. When trekking from Bjorli into the Tafjord mountains, various trails lead to the mountain huts of Friisbua to the south west,

Pyttbua to the west, past Tunga seter, Vakkerstøylen to the north west on the shores of Ulvådalsvatnet, and the Veltdal hut, south west of Pyttbua. One of the most popular walks in this area is a three day route from Bjorli to Tafjord via the summit of Pytteggen (Route 291). The 1:50,000 map for the area is the Tafjordfjella Turkart.

Pytteggen 1,999m (6,597ft)

The only mountain in Romsdal county where your head (if not your feet) will be over 2000m when standing on the summit! Iver Gjelstenli in his guide *Fra topp til Topp i Romsdal* says that spring ski-tours in the

Pytteggen area are Romsdal's answer to the Haute Route.

289. EAST RIDGE
(Party unknown)

A long mountain excursion of no difficulty but with excellent views from Romsdal's highest top. About 5 hours from Pyttbua. Grade I.

From Bjorli, take the road westwards to Tungaseter at the foot of Ulvedals Lake and follow the path south west for about 7km to Pyttbua hut. From the hut continue by the cairned path which crosses the river from North Hånådalsbotn, then ascend straight up the east ridge (snow).

290. DESCENT BY THE EAST RIDGE
(Party unknown)

This is a continuation of the above route, down to the lodge at Reindal seter. About 3 hours.

From the summit, descend the east ridge until it is possible to contour round beneath the south face, with 'steep black walls like a fortress with towers and bastions'. Continue west down the valley between Pytteggen and Høgstolen to the uppermost Reindals Lake and so, by the cairned path, to Reindalseter.

291. WALK FROM BJORLI TO TAFJORD

This 32km walk passes both Pyttbua Hut and Reindalseter. From the car park at Tunga seter, follow the trail along the line of the river for 10km to Pyttbua. From here, the path continues west then south for 15km to Reindalseter, or you have the option to ascend to Romsdal's highest top, Pytteggen via the East Ridge (see above). From Reindalseter, it's another 7km west via Sakrisvatn to the road which goes down to Tafjord (private bus service).

Alternatively, from Reindalseter a return journey can be done:

292. WALK ROUND PYTTEGGEN

From Reindalseter, return to Pyttbua first by walking south east for about 10km to Veltdalseter on the lake shore, then another 8km north east on the path back to Pyttbua, passing east of Karitind. The gap between Helleho and Karitind is called Kariløyft and provides an interesting passage.

Karitind 1,982m (6,541ft)

Situated between Pytteggen (to its north west) and Benkehø, its west ridge is said to have possibilities for climbing but there are no reports.

293.

Ascend from Pyttbua. 3–4 hours

294.

Karitind can also be reached from Reindalseter either via Veltdalseter or directly, then down to Veltdal. Grade I.

Benkehø 1,900m (6,432ft)

This summit is between Friisbua and Pyttbua huts.

295.

From Friisbua walk to the col between Helleho and Benkehø and then up to the top. The ascent is only a scramble. Grade I.

Descent Return by the same route and follow the north side of the valley down. The river can be crossed by a bridge at the confluence of the Hånådalsbotn rivers, close to Pyttbua.

Dovrefjell

Though actually outside Romsdal county, the Dovre massif borders its south east. It dominates the E6 road to Oppdal and Trondheim from Dombås and, like the Tafjord mountains, is easily reached from there. It is therefore convenient for walkers visiting nearby Pytteggen (see above) or en route either from the Rondane mountains just to the south, or to Romsdal. Here are some of Norway's highest summits outside the Jotunheim. Highest of all is Snøhetta, the highest summit in this guide. Its lower slopes are home to a herd of muskox, magnificent ice-age animals, which wander the wild terrain adding a unique attraction.

There is some climbing on Snøhetta, in the obvious couloirs rising from the snow filled, glaciated corrie below the summit, but the region is best known for its popular trails, some described in *Walking in Norway* (Cicerone Press). All are well served by DNT huts, mostly self service as well as private ones. The map to the area (which extends west to Eikesdal) is Dovrefjell Turkart 1:100,000.

Most people visiting here will start from Kongsvoll (reached by road or rail). It is ideally situated for Snøhetta and the muskox. The old lodge at Kongsvoll is 300 years old and stands on the ancient Pilgrim's Way over Dovrefjell. It's origins date back to the 12th century when King Øystein had a shelter built here. Close to the hotel, there is a natural alpine garden, which is well worth seeing to get a better understanding of the unique flora of the area.

Snøhetta 2,286m (7,545ft)

Walkers with only a day to spare can spend it happily on the plateau below Snøhetta, reached using the approach below. They are likely to be rewarded with views of muskox as well as having a wonderful day in wild scenery. Those wishing to reach the summit will require a little longer:

296. KONGSVOLL TO SNØHETTA

About 25km to the top, with an overnight stay at the Reinheim self service hut reached in 16km. The path starts at Kongsvoll, crosses the railway just up the road to the left, and then rises up through flower-filled birch woods onto the once glaciated high moors with their tumbling streams, moraines, eskers and kettle-holes dating back 20,000 years to the last ice age. From the Reinheim hut, continue to Snøhetta on day two, from where one can return to Reinheim (about 9km) for a second night, then back to Kongsvoll. Alternatively, continue via Åmotsdalshytte and Gammelseter to Gjøra, 35km to the north on the Sunndalsøra road.

Various other routes continue north into the Trollheimen area or west to Eikesdal and Romsdal. A possible trek from Romsdal to Dovre has already been mentioned (Route 34).

Snøhetta from the east

Winter Ice-Climbs

The gash of Hall's Renne, Romsdalhorn, in winter. The two dots at bottom centre are climbers

The summer season glacial ice climbs on Kalskratind, Kvandalstind and Finnan have already been described. Other than these and occasional treks across snowfields to reach the higher summits, snow and ice climbing in the Romsdal area is really a winter occupation.

Many of the big wall climbs and most, if not all, summits have had winter ascents. Additionally, in the last 20 years or so, a large number of other ice-climbs have also been done, predominantly on Romsdal's many frozen waterfalls. Here are the earliest routes. Others will be found in *Klatring i Romsdal.*

297. LILLETEIGSFOSSEN
(K Svanemyr, H Doseth. Jan. 1978)

A small ice climb almost in the centre of Åndalsnes. Two rope lengths. Starts with a vertical 3m section, the rest is at 60°.

298. SDOLÅA
(K Svanemyr, H Doseth. Dec. 1978)

The route is above Inholmen, after the last tunnel on the old coastal Ålesund road from Åndalsnes. It is the biggest and steepest of the streams. Six rope lengths. The first five are at about 75° with some vertical sections, whilst the last is the crux and involves a vertical 15m icicle.

299. SKOGAGROVA
(B Østigard, H Doseth. Feb 1978)

The ice is just opposite the big impressive waterfall called Dontefossen. About 2–3km above Flatmark just beside the road on the left side as seen from Åndalsnes. Six rope lengths at about 60°.

300. TROLLSTIGFOSSEN
(R Amundsen, H Doseth. Feb. 1978)

This is the famous waterfall at the head of the Isterdal Valley. Steepest section about 70° with easier climbing between. Six rope lengths.

301. TVERRELVA
(K Svanemyr, H Doseth. Feb 1978)

The waterfall left of Trollstigfossen. Eight rope lengths without the direct finish. Ice at about 60°–70°.

302. NYTTÅRSISEN
(H Doseth, K Svanemyr. Dec 1978)

Between Tverrelva and Trollstigfossen. The ice is just left of the bridge in Trollstigen. Nine short rope lengths at about 65°.

303. LEFT INNHOLMSICE
(K Svanemyr, H Doseth. Feb 1978)

This small stream is to the left of the big one just after the last of the three tunnels on the way to Ålesund from Åndalsnes. Eight rope lengths at about 60°.

304. NONSTIND WEST FLANK
(H Doseth, K Svanemyr. Mar 1978)

Takes an ice gully which runs up the outer edge of the face. The crux is a 15m, 75° ice-wall. On the top section the route goes just right of the big snow slope to the left of the top. Max 75°, 900m.

First winter ascent of Hall's Renne, 1981. *'One of the best ice routes on Romsdalshorn'*

Some Useful Anglo-Norwegian Words

MOUNTAINS

Abseil	Nedfiring
Aiguille	Syltopp
Arête	Egg
Avalanche	Skred
Axe	Øks
Belay	Forankring
Bergschrund	Bergschrund
Boulder	Steine
Boulder slope	Steinur, Storur
Brook	Bekk, Elv
Buttress	Knaus, Hammer
Cairn	Varde
Cave	Hule
Chasm	Kløft
Chimney	Skorstein
(rounded)	Nut
Cirque	Botn
Cleft	Hakk, Kløft
Cliff	Stup
Col	Skar
Corner	Hjørne
Cornice	Snøkant, Iskant
Couloir	Fjellkløft
Crack	Rift, Sprekk
Crag	Knaus, Hammer
Crampon	Ispigg
Crest	Fjellkamm
Crevasse	Bresprekk
Dale	Dal
Dam	Damm, Demning
Diedre	Hjørne
Escarpment	Skarning
Gap (narrow)	Kløft
Gendarme	Pinnakel
Ghyll	Gjel, Juv
Glacier	Bre
Glen	Fjelldal
Gorge	Gjel, Slukt
Groove	Renne
Gully	Renne
Headland	Nes

Hill	Haug, Bakke
Hut	Hytte
Ice	Is
Ice-axe	Isøks
Ice fall	Isfall
Lake	Vatn, Sjø
Ledge	Hylle
Moraine	Morene
Mountain	Fjell
Needle	Nål
Overhang	Hang, Utforheng
Pass	Fjellpass
Peak (sharp)	Tind
Pillar	Pilar
Pinnacle	Nål, Pigg, Tagg
Pitch	Strekk
Plateau	Fly, Platå
Piton	Bolt
Precipice	Stup
Rescue	Redning
Ridge(broad)	Rygg
Ridge (long)	Kjøl, Kamm
Ridge (sharp)	Egg
River	Elv
Rock	Fjell, Stein
Rope	Tau
Route	Rute
Rucksack	Ryggsekk
Scree	Bratt, Gruslende
Shoulder	Aksla
Fjord	Fjord
Slab	Sva, Flag
Snow	Snø, Sne
Stream	Bekk, Elv
(wide)	Band
Summit	Topp
Tarn	Vatn
Tower	Tårn
Traverse	Traversere

Valley	Dal
Wall	Vegg
Waterfall	Foss

WEATHER

Dawn	Soloppgang
Fog	Take
Heat	Varme
Midday	Mid dag
Midnight sun	Midnattsol
Mist	Skodde
Rain	Regne
Rainbow	Regnebue
Sleet	Sludd
Storm	Storm
Sunshine	Solskinn
Sunset	Solnedgang
Twilight	Skumring
Weather	Vaer
(bad)	Uvaer
(good)	God vaer

DESCRIPTIVE TERMS

Bad	Dårlig
Better	Bedre
Conical	Konisk
Fine	Fin
Good	God
Great	Stor
High(er)	Høg(re)
Highest	Høgst

Large	Stor
Little	Lille
Low(er)	Lav(ere)
Lowest	Lavest
Rough	Ujampt
Slippery	Sleip
Steep	Bratt
Worse	Vaerre
Worst	Vaerst

DIRECTIONAL TERMS

Ascend	Klatre
Back	Tilbake
Central	Midtre
Descend	Stige ned
Diagonal	Diagonal
Down	Ned
East	Øst
Eastern	Østlig
Forwards	Fram
Horizontal	Vannrett
Left	Venstre
Level	Rett
Middle	Midtre
North	Nord
Northern	Nordre
Right	Høire
South	Sør
Southern	Søndre
Up	Opp
Vertical	Loddrett
West	Vest
Western	Vestlig

Index of Peaks

Adelsfjell	109
Agottinder	40
Aksla (Nesaksla)	56
Benkehø	137
Bispen	116
Blånebba	60
Blåstolen	134
Breitind	77
Bjørka	105
Brudgommen	102
Brura	101
Brurjentene	101
Brur Skar	101

Dronninga	124
Finnan	129
Fløtatind	40
Goksøyra	37
Grønfonntind	133
Hauduken	41
Haukelutind	41
Hesten	133
Hoemstind	41
Holstind	61
Hornaksla	69

Juratind 41

Kalskratind 70
Karitind 137
Karitind (South ranges) 119
Klauva 46
Kleneggen 40
Klumpen 85
Kongen 118
Kvandalstind 52
Kyrketaket 46

Lille Hesten 133
Lille Romsdalshorn 66
Lille Skjorta 39
Lille Vengetind 51

Måsevasstind 134
Middagsfjell 131
Middagstind (Finnan Group) 131
Middagstind (West Ranges) 134
Midtre Agottind 40
Midtre Finnan 129
Mjølva 57
Moanebba 47
Mongejura 72

Nesaksla (Aksla) 56
Nonstind 134
Norafjell 110
Nordre Trolltind 106
Nyheitind 42

Olaskartind 70

Princessa Pinnacle 125
Pyteggen 136

Ringshorn 132
Romsdalshorn 62

Semletind (Søndre Trolltind) 80
Seterfjell 133
Setergjeitind 112
Setnesfjell 125
Sjødala 42
Skarven 44
Skjorta 39
Søndre Trolltind 80
Snøhetta 138
Spørsmålstegnet 102
Stabben 85
Stighorn (Stigbotnhorn) 112

Store Trolltind 102
Store Vengetind 48
Storfjell 133
Storgrovfjell 112
Strandfjell 45
Søndre Finnan 129
Søndre Trolltind 80
Søre Vengetind 52
Søstrene 105

Taskedalstind 133
Trollgubben 101
Trollkjerringa 101
Trollklørne 105
Trollryggen 85
Trollspiret 100
Trollstølen 134
Trollvasstind 134

Ugla 102

Vikesaksa 40

Østre Finnan 130

Index of Peaks